The Age of Capitalism and Bureaucracy

The Age of Capitalism and Bureaucracy

Perspectives on the Political Sociology of Max Weber

Second, Expanded Edition

Wolfgang J. Mommsen

berghahn
NEW YORK · OXFORD
www.berghahnbooks.com

First published in 1974 by Blackwell

Second edition published in
2021 by Berghahn Books

© 2021 Sabine Mommsen

Library of Congress Cataloging-in-Publication Data

A C.I.P. cataloging record is available from the Library of Congress
Library of Congress Cataloging in Publication Control Number:
2021938121

British Library Cataloguing in Publication Data

A catalogue record for this book is available from the British Library

ISBN 978-1-80073-079-3 hardback
ISBN 978-1-80073-126-4 paperback
ISBN 978-1-80073-080-9 ebook

Contents

Foreword by Volker R. Berghahn   vi

Preface to the First Edition   xiv

List of Abbreviations   xvii

Introduction   1

Chapter 1. The Universal Historian and the Social Scientist   5

Chapter 2. The Champion of Nationalist Power Politics and Imperialism   22

Chapter 3. The Alternative to Marx: Dynamic Capitalism instead of Bureaucratic Socialism   41

Chapter 4. The Theory of the 'Three Pure Types of Legitimate Domination' and the Concept of Plebiscitarian Democracy   60

Chapter 5. A Liberal in Despair   77

Bibliography: The Main Works of Max Weber   93

Postscript by Volker R. Berghahn   98

Select Bibliography   117

Index   119

Foreword

Volker R. Berghahn

Max Weber continues to rank among the most important social scientists of modern industrial societies. Although he died more than one hundred years ago, his work and his conceptualizations are still as relevant to the world of the twenty-first century as they were to the earlier periods that he made the focus of his research and writings. The trouble is that these writings are so voluminous and complex that it had become difficult to see the wood for the trees. Wolfgang Mommsen has been widely recognized as one of the foremost experts on Weber, and it was the strength and virtue of his book on the age of bureaucracy and capitalism, first published in 1974, that it explained basic concepts of Weber's interpretation of the modern world very concisely in a little over 110 pages. However, a brief glance at the table of contents will show that this book is not merely concerned with Weber's thought on these two topics. There is a chapter on Weber's development as an academic from the late nineteenth century to the First World War. Knowing that Weber was never just a researcher who surveyed the world from the ivory tower, but explicitly engaged in contemporary debates on German society and politics from the 1890s all the way to the military defeat and collapse of the Hohenzollern monarchy in the revolutionary upheavals of 1918/19, Mommsen also discusses Weber's attitudes towards German nationalism and its relationship with the imperialist ambitions that the country's political, economic, and cultural elites developed around the turn of the century.

There is furthermore an important chapter on Weber's engagement with Marxism as the great rival system to his own analysis of modern capitalism and its origins. With Weber being concerned with the uses of power when it came to discussions about the future of Western societies, Mommsen rightly felt that he had to devote another chapter to an explication of what Weber meant when he wrote about the 'three pure types of legitimate domination'. In his final chapter Mommsen returns to Weber's somber thoughts about the future and his sense that Western civilization was headed towards a state of increasing bureaucratization. He feared that we would all be dominated by the expert and were destined to end up in an 'iron cage of serfdom'. But, as will be seen in a moment, he did not give up hope of a different longer-term development through which liberal individualism and creativity would survive.

Mommsen knew that he faced a considerable challenge when he tried to compress Weber's extensive and not always coherent and lucid writings into a slim volume, and then to convert his own complex sentences into the English language whose structural principles are quite different from German prose. This is why this new Introduction to this book aims to provide a few guidelines on the contemporary societal context within which Weber pondered and wrote about the big issues of his time. There is also a further and more pragmatic consideration underlying the reissue of Wolfgang Mommsen's study. It relates to the ways courses designed to introduce students to the concepts and methods of the disciplines of History and Sociology, tend to take very recent studies that supposedly contain 'cutting-edge' knowledge of particular specialized sub-field. This approach can be mesmerizing to the budding historian or social scientist, keen to learn about recent research, but it suffers from one pitfall: he/she does not get a sense of the historical evolution of their chosen discipline. There is also much plausibility in the argument that there are few questions that earlier generations have in one way or another not grappled with before and thus continue to be the basis of many issues that are still with us today. In this respect there can be little doubt that Max Weber's writings are among those that both undergraduates and graduate students will find helpful as they read about the complexities and challenges of the modern world.

The purpose of reissuing Mommsen's study is to present Weber in terms of some of the major questions that preoccupied him as one of the towering social scientists of his time. His volume also presents an analysis of a number of key concepts of Weber's thought and the insights that can be gained from them, as we deal with the structures and dynamics of modern industrial societies. If the following chapters whet the reader's appetite for more, it should be relatively easy to get hold of some of the titles listed in the short bibliography at the end and to look online for Weber's books and the scholarly literature in English or German about his life and work.

Mommsen's first chapter traces Weber's intellectual journey in the late nineteenth century and before 1914 when he was still under the influence of History – at the time the dominant discipline in the humanities at German universities. However, in those days historians were still primarily concerned with politics, political elites, decision-makers and the projection of national power at home and abroad. In other words, the focus was on the nation state and its origins that some historians complemented by a quest to identify transnational and universalist forces in human history. However, these were also the decades when some historians became interested in questions of economy, society and culture. Well familiar with these academic currents, Weber was never a narrow specialist who would pursue just one topic in depth to become the world authority in a chosen field. Instead he immersed himself in many if not all of them and became particularly interested in problems of political, socio-economic and cultural power.

In the 1890s, Weber was not only more of a historian than a social scientist, but also an intellectual with strong views on contemporary issues. Thus he created quite a sensation in 1894 when, after his appointment to a professorship of economics at Freiburg University, he used his inaugural lecture to pose as an ardent German nationalist who argued that the country must assert itself among the major powers of the world.[1] Indeed, he went so far as to claim that the founding of the Bismarckian empire in 1871 would have been a futile endeavor, unless it took its place among the great powers of the world. In an international system that, in his eyes, was based on Social Darwinist principles of the survival of the fittest, Weber advocated not peaceful trade or the informal commercial penetration of other countries, but the forceful acquisition of overseas territories. Given the aggressive imperialist policies that Germany adopted under Emperor Wilhelm II and in the 1930s and 1940s under Hitler, it is distressing to read Weber's lectures and articles during the Kaiserreich. Worse, they also contain racist undertones, directed mainly against the Slavic populations in the East who had been attracted as cheap migrant labor to work on the large estates of the Prussian landowners after the German-born laborers had moved westward. The latter had been leaving the East to escape economic and political exploitation by these landlords and looked for comparatively better conditions of employment and life in the expanding industrial regions, especially of the Rhineland.

Without condoning Weber's prejudices on these questions, it is nevertheless striking how immersed he was in the intellectual discourses among the academic elites of this time that, in turn, had become part of the ideology of an upward mobile commercial-industrial and cultural bourgeoisie. It was this stratum that had greatly benefitted from the growing prosperity of the boom years around the turn to the twentieth century and that had begun to demand a greater share of the power concentrated in the hands of a conservative and increasingly reactionary monarchical government and its supporters among the Prussian landowning class. Add to these developments the achievements in the sciences and humanities and what has been called *Die Entzauberung der Welt* ('disenchantment of the world'),[2] and it becomes comprehensible why so many of Weber's colleagues, bursting with pride and longing for social recognition, espoused nationalist and imperialist ideas. In fairness, it should be added, though, that the positions that Weber took up in the 1890s were not immutable. After the turn of the century he moderated his positions and distanced himself from his earlier racism. If he had at one point supported the views of the Pan-German League, he now became a critic of Wilhelmine foreign and domestic policy. Once the First World War had been unleashed by the two Central European monarchies and Weber witnessed the catastrophic impact of total war, he was among the advocates of peace negotiations, however slim their chances of success. He also opposed the Treaty of Brest-Litovsk that, following the collapse of Tsarist Russia, the German government imposed on the revolutionary Bolshevik regime in order to annex huge territories in the Ukraine, also in a futile attempt to turn the tide in Germany's favor on the embattled Western front in France.

Closely observing the course of world history after the beginning of the twentieth century, Weber's scholarly concerns shifted increasingly away from historical studies. He distanced himself from his History colleagues who were primarily interested in narratives derived from archival sources and kept tracing causal connections in the past. He began to argue with them about their claims that this past could be retrieved quite simply from a meticulous evaluation of documents in the archives, a method that allegedly enabled them to reconstruct what had 'really happened'. Nor did Weber consider their notion of *Verstehen* sufficient; to him all serious research invariably required critical scrutiny. Instead of mere story-telling Weber insisted on a more systematic analysis of the world around him. By this time it had also become impossible to ignore, as most of his History colleagues had done, the role of the impoverished working class in the development of modern industrial societies, which led Weber to the study of Marxism that had been such a crucial propellant of the mobilization and organization of the German working class before 1914. Although he agreed with Karl Marx that viewing modern industrial society in terms its class conflicts was insightful, he disagreed with his sweeping interpretation of the whole of human history in dialectical terms. At the same time, he was intrigued by Marx's focus on the role of capitalism as a driving force of historical change during past centuries, but then came up with an alternative conception of its dynamism. Weber asserted that human behavior was not exclusively determined by a person's 'hard' purely socio-economic position within a capitalist class structure, but also by perceptions and self-perceptions of social status and rank, i.e., factors that were less tangible and more cultural in comparison to Marx's economic notions of class. It is along this latter line of argument that Weber arrived at a major reinterpretation of capitalism. If Marx, rejecting the Hegelian position that ideas were the motor of History, had supposedly put Hegel on its feet by postulating that an individual's material situation determined his (or more implicitly her) consciousness, Weber came along claiming that it was consciousness that determined being.

It is from this base that Weber began to define the rise of modern capitalism in Europe. While for Marxists it was the dialectic of socio-economic class struggle between the owners of the means of production and the exploited working class, for Weber capitalism was the outgrowth of a new mental attitude towards economic activity that he saw emerging in Europe among the Puritans during the early modern period. To them economic activity was not sinful and one that could only find redemption in another, transcendental world of divine forgiveness. Rather it was virtuous to be economically creative, to live an ascetic life, and to be successful as an individual in this world. Recognition was then assured not only in this life, but would also be given in the after-life. It is in this larger religious-philosophical context that Weber's seminal study of modern capitalism has to be seen, with its highly significant title: *The Protestant Ethic[!] and the Spirit[!] of Capitalism*.[3] The title gives Weber's interpretation of capitalism away, if combined with his notion of the simultaneous rise of rationalism that in Weber's view reached beyond the bounds of soberly calculating economic activity. To him, there was a much broader *Entzauberung* of the world and a concomitant decline of the power of ideology. What he postulated, seems to introduce a teleological element in his understanding of modern occidental society. Other experts have focused on those references in Weber's writings that seem to point to an underlying evolutionary view of world that was in line with nineteenth-century liberalism and Weber's concern with how humans conducted their lives more generally rather than merely as *homini oeconomici*.

There is yet another point that is important for an understanding of Weber's view of capitalism. If by 1900 the United States had become the country of capitalist modernity that European entrepreneurs visited to study its organizations and production methods, he, too, sailed across the Atlantic in 1904.[4] But, apart from inspecting a few of the centres of American industrial capitalism and attending the World Exhibition in St. Louis where the participant nations displayed, through the architecture of their pavilions and their manufactures, how they saw themselves in the new century, he also spent time to study the welter of Protestant sects and movements around which the socio-economic and cultural-religious life in communities throughout the American continent was organized. It is here that he witnessed a competitive plurality of not only rational economic behavior, but also of daily human conduct and socio-cultural interaction within those communities.

If these are the broad parameters of Weber's conception of capitalism, it is not surprising that he became a life-long critic of Marxism, even if both interpretations had their roots in the Enlightenment and both men saw capitalism as a product of the age of rationalism and economic calculation. Still, Weber thought Marx's interpretation of human history in terms of class conflicts that unfolded as a Law of History and in which the confrontation between industrial workers and capitalist entrepreneurs was merely the most recent stage was misguided. Nor did he accept Marx's vision that, after the predicted collapse of capitalism from its inner contradictions as well as the revolutionary struggle of the proletariat, human history would find its culmination point in a classless communist society that had overcome past conflicts and was at peace with itself. Marx's view that domination of men by men would disappear was simply utopian to Weber. There were no definitive cyclical termini, nor were societal developments linear or irrevocable. Finally, Weber rejected the notion that centralized economic planning was the best method of securing a fair and equitable distribution of goods, ending poverty and starvation, and that planning would also take care of adequate social-security provisions for health, child care, and pensions for the elderly. Weber, by contrast, believed that the market was the best place for the distribution of goods and for securing the livelihoods and housing needs of the population at large. For him, capitalism was based on the private ownership of creative individuals who would uphold the principle of competition not only against state intervention, but also against attempts to establish powerful private monopoly positions.

This did not mean that Weber had abandoned his earlier view that the ability to project and maintain power was basic to human existence and assertion. In the 1890s, his writings and lectures had still revolved around nationalism and imperial expansion. But the distribution of power in its political, economic, and cultural guise, was also crucial to his understanding of the internal structures and evolution of a national society. The question was how to make certain that power was not abused or its use did not degenerate into an autocratic monarchy or a populist dictatorship. This leads to Mommsen's chapter relating to Weber's theory of the 'Three Pure Types of Legitimate Domination'. That these types should be called 'pure' points to his shift away from History and its methods to that of the sociology and the development of intellectual constructs. What he called an 'ideal type' amounted to an assembly of factors that could be used as yardsticks to be held against the available empirical material to gauge how far the actual object of research matched or diverged from the approximations of the 'pure' ideal type. For example, Weber would compile a list of criteria that were deemed typical of modern bureaucracy, such as its hierarchical structures, promotion by seniority, or life-long service with guaranteed pension rights at the end, etc. These criteria could then be pitched against the actual empirical evidence of a particular national or local bureaucracy.

However, Weber was not just interested in how accurately a chosen case study compared to his pre-constructed 'ideal type' bureaucracy; there was also the question of how power was distributed within it or, even more importantly, within a particular society and how, above all, it was legitimated. For Weber it was axiomatic that *Herrschaft*, as he called it and that is translated by Mommsen as 'domination', required legitimation by which he meant that it had to be freely accepted by those who were dominated. Where this legitimation was not given or refused, autocratic imposition or revolt and ensuing instability and chaos were the alternatives. It is from these fundamental premises that Weber developed his 'three pure types of legitimate domination' that he called traditional, legal-bureaucratic and charismatic. The table on pp. 62–63 provides a list of how he broke down and classified the three types. Looking at them historically, it was clear that both 'charismatic' and 'traditional' domination had existed in earlier centuries and that the latter was on its way out under the pressures of economic, political and cultural modernization that rational capitalism had been exerting on monarchical rule since its emergence in the sixteenth century. Instead the modern period had seen the rise of 'legal' or bureaucratic domination.

It is at this point that there emerges another ambiguity in Weber's analysis of capitalism and bureaucracy. On the one hand and perhaps exacerbated by his illness and the international upheavals around him, he shared the kind of cultural pessimism that was widespread in intellectual and academic circles in Central Europe after 1900. What in this respect worried him most was the rise of the expert and of bureaucracies that were encroaching upon both the public and private sectors of society and that even supposedly dynamic capitalist enterprises had become exposed to bureaucratization and routinization, leading Weber to believe that we were increasingly dominated by bureaucrats, by the *Fachmenschen*.

Worse, having experienced and witnessed the collapse of traditional monarchies and modern authoritarian administrations, Weber was concerned that personal political, economic and cultural freedoms would become increasingly restricted. In his most pessimistic moments he feared that in the age of rational capitalism and of the expanding administrative state Western societies end up in the above-mentioned 'iron cage of serfdom', perhaps still enjoying a level of consumerist prosperity, but under illiberal political conditions. Accordingly, Mommsen calls Weber a 'liberal in despair' who is afraid that the dynamic of modern public and private bureaucracies would overwhelm liberal individualism that he regarded as indispensable also to the freedom of intellectual debate and scholarship. But his position is not clear-cut. He also believed that the future was more open and that an alternative industrial society might be conceivable, propelled through his third type of legitimate domination: charismatic leadership, legitimated by a 'plebiscitarian democracy'. While Weber did not live to see the rise of charismatic leaders in the 1920s and 1930s who based their domination on populist acclamation, it is his toying with this particular way out of the dilemma of Western modernity that is why his ideal-typical conceptualization came under severe criticism after his passing. By the 1930s, he was seen by some social scientists and politicians as the intellectual precursor of Italian Fascism and German National Socialism.

But when he conceptualized a 'plebiscitarian democracy', Weber – as Mommsen stressed – was not thinking of a future in which the pseudo-democratic regimes that Adolf Hitler and Benito Mussolini would use to destroy the type of society Weber had had in mind while he was still alive. In fact he continued to operate intellectually within the constitutional-parliamentary framework of the nineteenth century that had produced not only capitalist rationality but also charismatic leaders from within. He did not envisage a dictator, but leaders who, legitimated by a democratic-representative political system, would be entrusted by their voters with the reins of government to deal with a serious crisis in an effort to counter, contain and weaken, if only ephemerally, the structures of bureaucratic domination. Whatever the dangers that threatened creative and value-oriented humanity, in the end the 'liberal in despair' thus saw a ray of hope whose strength will be assessed in the Postscript of this book that looks at the age of capitalism and bureaucracy since Weber's death.

Notes

1. See Wolfgang J. Mommsen, *Max Weber und die deutsche Politik, 1890–1920*, Tübingen 1959.
2. Max Weber, *The Protestant Ethic and the Spirit of Capitalism*, London 1965.
3. See Andreas Daum, *Wissenschaftspopularisierung im 19. Jahrhundert. Bürgerliche Kultur, naturwissenschaftliche Bildung und die deutsche Öffentlichkeit, 1848–1914*, Munich 1998.
4. See, e.g., Lawrence A. Scaff, *Max Weber in America*, Princeton 2011. He was accompanied by his wife Marianne who was a writer and activist for women's emancipation and who, in her time, was better known in Germany than her husband. She published her account of their trip much later in 1926. On these visits to 'The New World' more generally and German business interest in the United States, see, e.g., Mary Nolan, *Visions of Modernity. American Business and the Modernization of Germany*, New York 1994. See also Stefan Breuer, 'Classe, ceto e strato nella sociologia della religione di Max Weber,' in: *Scienza & Politica*, No. 63 (2020), 41–61, for a clarification of Weber's uses of class and status, especially after 1909, but with the main focus on religious stratification.

Preface to the First Edition

This book was written in the hope that it might give an additional stimulus to the revival of interest in Max Weber which can be observed in the English-speaking world at this moment. It may help a little to make people realize that Max Weber was much more than a great empirical social scientist. The importance of his thinking at the present juncture of Western thought lies mainly in the fact that throughout his sociological and political work he always reflected the significance of his particular findings for the future course of mankind. It was his still unsurpassed knowledge of the past history of human societies which gave him an acute perception of the key issues of his own age. He was a sociologist who never allowed himself to become a prey to social analysis, devoted only to short term problems, and the obvious conservative bias usually associated with such an approach. He was concerned with some of the most pressing problems of his age, in particular the rise of bureaucratic social structures which would eventually leave no more room for the spontaneous, creative activity of individuals who are motivated by the highest values of a very personal nature. He worked hard to enlighten people's minds, and to suggest solutions which might enable the individual to hold his own against the rise of seemingly omnipotent bureaucracies, and to help western societies to hold in check those social forces which were about to suffocate silently, but remorselessly the liberal individualistic social structures of his day. It may well be said that half a century after Max Weber's premature death most of these problems are still with us even though we sometimes see them in a different light.

This interpretation of Max Weber's political sociology is at least in part a response to the challenge of presenting his political and sociological ideas to English-speaking audiences during several visits to English and American universities. The very different intellectual tradition of the Anglo-Saxon world, as compared with the German, and its pragmatic conception of the role of the state in society, contrasted with the Hegelian tradition in Germany, have to no small degree influenced even the language itself. To write about Max Weber in English hence has a stimulating effect; many key issues appear in a new light. Also one is forced to pay attention to problems which, in the German language (and the general intellectual framework associated with it) would pass almost unnoticed. Visits to the Institute of Advanced Study in Princeton in 1968 and to St. Antony's, College in Oxford in 1971–72 enabled me to discuss the problems involved with many colleges and students. For valuable suggestions I am indebted, above all, to Steven Lukes, Melvin Richter, and Philip Rieff. Earlier drafts of the last chapter were presented in 1969 at the Institute of Advanced Study in Princeton, N.J., as well as at the University of California at Berkeley, and in a public lecture delivered in Oxford on 4 February 1972. The main theses were made the subject of a seminar on 'Max Weber as a Universal Historian and Political Thinker' which was held at St. Antony's College, Oxford, during the Michaelmas term of 1972. I should like to express my thanks to all those who made the seminar possible, in particular the Warden and Fellows of St. Antony's College who invited me to come to Oxford as a guest professor for two terms, and to the Volkswagen Foundation which made the Volkswagen Professorship in Modern German History at St. Antony's possible through its generous financial support. Otherwise this book would probably not have been written at all. Furthermore my thanks must go to Anthony Nicholls, Fellow of St. Antony's College, and Timothy Mason, Fellow of St. Peter's College, Oxford, who were always ready to help me whenever there were any difficulties; without their assistance and advice this book could not have been realized. Apart from that I should like to thank Miss Abley for her efficiency and her unlimited patience in finding me all the books which I needed. The librarians of Nuffield College very kindly made available to me some key publications about Max Weber which were not easily to be found elsewhere.

It is always a considerable risk for an author to write a book in a language which is not his mother tongue. Even if the reader finds it not always elegant in style, the fact that he may find it comprehensible, is mainly due to Miss Jane Hilbert of St. Antony's College, Oxford, who took pains to revise the original drafts with great patience and remarkable empathy, and above all to Mr. J. Feather of Blackwell who undertook the arduous task of editing. I hope, however, that the remaining linguistic shortcomings are somewhat offset by a comparatively precise rendering of Max Weber's thoughts in English. One should always bear in mind that Max Weber's texts make unusually difficult reading even in the original, and that it often requires a penetrating analysis to put the correct meaning of a particular passage into readable English. As the author has for long been intimately familiar with the published as well as most of the unpublished writings of Weber, he thinks it sensible to try to take advantage of this, and to present

Max Weber to English readers with a maximum of precision, although the results are often anything but elegant, and at times make difficult reading. Even so I flatter myself that I have done my best to communicate to an English audience Max Weber's passionate striving for terminological precision as well as his scrupulous, and often almost pedantic struggle to present the issues from all conceivable points of view and at the same time with the greatest possible exactitude.

For this reason I felt free to deviate from the available English editions of Weber's works, whenever the translation seemed to be either too loose, or not to render a particular point with sufficient clarity. This does not mean that Weber's translators have not done a good job; obviously translating a great author, particularly if he writes with so sophisticated a diction, means at the same time interpreting him. However, in order to enable the reader to check the exact meaning of the quotations for himself, the corresponding English translation is always cited alongside the original German version. Other references, however, were kept within limits; only in special cases is my point of view defended in detail against the views of other scholars on the subject. A bibliography at the end of this volume lists the main works of Max Weber as well as the more relevant and more recent literature. We hope that it may serve as a useful guide for the English reader in finding his way through the vast literature.

Wolfgang J. Mommsen, October 1972

Abbreviations

Bendix	Reinhard Bendix, *Max Weber. An Intellectual Portrait*, New York, 1960.
EaS	*Economy and Society. An Outline of Interpretive Society*, ed. Günther Roth and Claus Wittich, New York, 1968.
Gerth	*From Max Weber. Essays in Sociology*, Trans. and ed. H. H. Gerth and C. Wright Mills, 6 ed., London, 1967.
Lebensbild	Marianne Weber, *Max Weber. Ein Lebensbild*, Neudruck Heidelberg, 1950.
Mommsen, *Max Weber*	Wolfgang J. Mommsen, *Max Weber und die deutsche Politik, 1890–1920*, Tübingen, 1959.
Mommsen, *Universalgeschichtliches Denken*	Wolfgang J. Mommsen, 'Universalgeschichtliches und politisches Denken bei Max Weber', *Historische Zeitschrift*, Vol. 201, 1965.
Mommsen, *Plebiszitäre Führerdemokratie*	Wolfgang J. Mommsen, Zum Begriff der 'plebiszitären Führerdemokratie' bei Max Weber, *Kölner Zeitschrift für Soziologie und Sozialpsychologie*, Vol. 20, 1969.
PS	*Gesammelte politische Schriften*, 3. ed., Tübingen, 1968.
Shils	*Max Weber on the Methodology of the Social Sciences*, ed. Edward A. Shils and Henry A. Finch, Glencoe, Ill., 1949.
SSP	*Gesammelte Aufsätze zur Soziologie und Sozialpolitik*, Tübingen, 1924.

WL	*Gesammelte Aufsätze zur Wissenschaftslehre,* 3 ed., Tübingen, 1968.
WuG	*Wirtschaft und Gesellschaft. Grundriß der verstehenden Soziologie,* 4 ed., Tübingen, 1956.

Introduction

In this book the fundamental aspects of Max Weber's political sociology are discussed in the light of his personal views about the course of world history. The central issues of his sociological works as well as of his political thought are without exception related to his growing anxiety about the future of the liberal societies of the west, in an age of rapidly expanding bureaucracies. He was convinced that the universal advance of bureaucratic forms of social and political organization was bound to place the principles of individual liberty and personal creativity in jeopardy. He perceived that the slow but steady ossification of the social systems in the west could only be prevented by social and political institutions which would guarantee maximum dynamism and leadership.

In the first chapter it is shown that Weber's sociological work is based on a specific concept of world history which is characterized by his liberal individualism as well as by an almost Nietzschean pessimism about the future of mankind. In fact, his sociological work and his political activities have a common origin, namely the passionate endeavour to fight for the preservation of a humane world endangered on the one hand by anachronistic political institutions, and on the other by the rise of all-powerful social forces which would allow less and less room for the autonomous individual and would render his personal set of values socially meaningless. Weber's encyclopaedic knowledge of world history enabled him to see the great social trends of his own age in a truly universal perspective, and to assess correctly their significance for western civilization. Although he gradually abandoned the historical approach, which is dominant in his earlier writings, in favour of a strictly formalized ideal-typical analysis of social phenomena, his scholarly work is substantially a historical sociology, as he in fact intended it to be. However detailed and sophisticated his various sociological studies are, they always reflect the socio-cultural significance of the respective social phenomena in a truly universal-historical perspective.

Max Weber's passionate championship of a German national imperialism seems at first sight to have little in common with his views about the future of western societies. In fact it even stands in strong contrast to his own conclusions about the nature of imperialism. Yet a close inspection reveals that Weber's imperialistic convictions are also embedded in this broad perspective of the future course of world history. In the final analysis Weber's liberal convictions strengthened his imperialistic zeal, at least in the 1890s. Weber thought that in the foreseeable future the nation state was likely to remain the basic unit of world politics, and hence he never hesitated as a citizen to identify himself with the political fortunes of his own nation. This was, in fact, totally compatible with his views about the role of nation states in history. The permanent struggle of the nation states against one another, whether through diplomatic or through economic means, was not only inevitable, but also a major source of political dynamism. However, he considered a high degree of dynamics and mobility to be essential ingredients of free, or, as they would be termed today, 'open' societies. Hence it was not unreasonable to identify himself with German 'world politics' on the one hand, and simultaneously to analyse the nature of imperialism in a thoroughly scholarly manner.

Absolutely central in Weber's thinking is the question of the social and cultural consequences of modern capitalism which he himself described as one of the great revolutionary forces in world history. Weber carefully researched into the origins of capitalism, and discovered that its rise was inseparably connected with those bourgeois values which were to be found in their purest form in Puritanism. He, indeed, was proud of this, and at times he demonstratively called himself 'a member of the bourgeois classes'. Yet, as is shown in the third chapter, Max Weber was anything but a blind partisan of modern capitalism. He analysed elaborately the social consequences of modern industrial capitalism, and he did not try to pass over its dehumanizing aspects. He pointed out that 'formal rationality' of capitalist institutions is necessarily associated with 'substantive irrationalities'; in this respect he largely anticipated Herbert Marcuse's criticism of the capitalist order. Yet he was firmly convinced that an easy alternative was not at hand. The solution suggested by Karl Marx was, in his opinion, incapable of solving the essential problem of how to preserve a maximum of individual freedom in industrial societies. Contrary to Marx he argued that the key issue was not the distribution of property, but the actual control of the managerial positions, for the latter rather than the former are the actual source of economic power. Therefore the nationalization of the means of production was unsuitable for the emancipation of the workers from 'alienation'; on the contrary it would make things worse, in as much as the workers would become the helpless prey of impersonal bureaucracies. Whatever the shortcomings of his position may have been otherwise, the truth of part of Weber's criticism of traditional Marxism has been shown by historical developments since his sudden death in 1920. It follows from this that Max Weber was a staunch defender of a competitive capitalist system. Although he did not deny that capitalism was very far from being the best of all possible systems, he thought that for the time being at least it deserved preference over all other possible economic systems, for it alone guaranteed maximum social mobility. Under given conditions capitalism presented the best chances for the preservation of individual freedom and creative leadership in a bureaucratic world.

In his political sociology as well as in his political writings Weber was, for much the same reasons, primarily concerned with the problems of leadership. His famous ideal-typical theory of 'three pure types of legitimate domination' classifies the various forms in which political authority is considered legitimate in the opinion of the ruled; yet it also shows that no government can altogether dispose of an element of personal rule. In the fourth chapter the problem is raised of how Weber's concept of parliamentary democracy fits into the theory of the 'three types of legitimate domination'. Surprisingly it turns out that democratic rule is defined by Weber in his context as an anti-authoritarian version of charismatic domination rather than as a value-rational version of legal domination. This has important consequences for the evaluation of Weber's concept of democracy.

In the last chapter these observations are integrated in a comprehensive interpretation of Max Weber's political philosophy. He considered the main question of his day to be how to check the rise of impersonal bureaucracies, and thus how to provide for effective leadership. Therefore he eventually turned to the extreme device of advocating what he called a 'plebiscitarian leader-democracy'. Great politicians with charismatic quality should help to preserve a maximum of mobility in bureaucratic structures. They ought to keep democracy alive in spite of bureaucratic institutions, and to infuse new aims into the social process on the basis of the confidence of the masses in their charismatic qualities. In other words, they ought continuously to challenge the thoughtless routine of the 'politicians without a calling', and thereby help to keep the 'open society' open, in the face of various social trends which pointed to the eventual emergence of omnipotent bureaucratic structures. Weber's recourse to the 'otherworldly'. power of charisma was by no means incidental; it was deeply rooted in his philosophy of history. He sincerely believed that there was no other means of fighting for a maximum of individual liberty and humanity in a bureaucratic age. It may well be that not all of his suggestions on how to solve the basic problems of western civilization will be accepted today. But he certainly raised key problems which have lost none of their importance during the five decades which separate us from his own lifetime.

CHAPTER 1

The Universal Historian
and the Social Scientist

To the English-speaking world Max Weber has always been presented in
bits and pieces, rather than in full. There are many anthologies, yet they
are highly selective; as a rule, they do not pay much attention to the respective position which the various texts contained in them had in the
context of Weber's scholarly work.[1] There is, however, not just 'one' Max
Weber; his works reveal many facets, and one can discern a distinctive
development in his methodological approach as well as in his substantive
work on the study of societies. It may be said that this point is not made
sufficiently clear either in Talcott Parsons's otherwise brilliant interpretation of Max Weber, or in Bendix's biography which looks at Max Weber
very much through the eyes of an empirical social scientist.[2]

It would seem to be almost impossible to do full justice to the scholarly
achievements of Max Weber by presenting him in one perspective only.
Yet it would be easier to discover the common thread which runs through
all his work, if a close look is taken at the various stages of his intellectual
development, giving particular attention to the underlying philosophical
conceptions. Max Weber's main aims, during a lifetime full of extreme
tensions and of constant attempts to live up to the principles of rational
conduct of a puritan cast, may perhaps best be summed up by saying that
he wanted to achieve two things, and both of them more or less at the
same time.

First, to present a genuinely *universal* interpretation of western civilization and of the 'uniqueness' (*Eigenart*) of its value systems as well as its
patterns of human behaviour. This was to be done by means of a comparative analysis of all sufficiently explored societies throughout the whole
history of mankind.

Secondly, to design adequate conceptual tools which would enable so-cial scientists to tackle the problems of present-day societies, and to help people to make rational choices in accordance with their personal sets of values, whatever the latter might be, by taking the possible, or, indeed, probable consequences of these very choices into consideration.

Weber's belief in sociology as a rational discipline was embedded, as may be gathered from his famous public lecture 'Science as a Vocation', in a very personal philosophy which had the dimension of a substantive ethic although he himself always shrank from trying to formulate the latter pos-itively and explicitly. This philosophy owed much to Friedrich Nietzsche if only with regard to the almost self-destroying radicalism with which Weber always tried to push whatever insights he had to the most extreme conclusion thinkable, or with regard to the almost complete disillusion concerning the existence of any objective values whatever: 'The fate of an epoch which has eaten of the tree of knowledge is that we must know that we cannot learn from the analysis of the world historical process, how-ever much this analysis may be perfected, anything about its intrinsic meaning – and that we have rather to create this meaning ourselves. We will have to realize that *"Weltanschauungen"* can never be the product of increasing empirical knowledge, and that, for this very reason, the highest ideals which move us most forcefully must always be realized in a struggle with other ideals which are just as sacred to others as ours are to us.'[3] From this it follows, moreover, that Max Weber was decidedly opposed to all sorts of speculative constructions of world history, or, to use Pop-per's famous phrase, 'holistic ideologies', whether they were descendants of Hegel and Marx or based on the romantic conception of a 'folk spirit' manifesting itself in the most diverse historical and cultural formations.

Yet, at the same time, Weber's own convictions rested on a specific conception of the nature of the world historical process, or to use a more general phrase, of universal history, although he himself never attempted to put it forward in an explicit theory.[4] It goes without saying that Max Weber was not a historian in the ordinary sense of the word, and he never claimed to be considered as one. On the other hand, his works display an abundance of historical knowledge which has so far not been surpassed by anyone else, with the possible exception of Arnold Toynbee. More than that, he was deeply influenced by German historicism, although he objected strongly to the idea that the historical process as such has an in-ner meaning which can be revealed by a close inspection of the historical sources. To the distress of Troeltsch he called the *Entwicklungsgedanken* a sheer 'romanticist swindle'.[5]

It has been argued recently by Emerich Francis and John Rex,[6] fol-lowing Carlo Antoni,[7] that Max Weber began his career as a historian of culture and that only relatively late in life – sometime around 1908 – did he turn towards sociology as a discipline concerned with general laws and theories of social change whilst previously he had tried to give interpretations of various social phenomena according to their 'cultural significance' (*Kulturbedeutung*), a term which is used often in Weber's earlier writings. Francis points out that, up to 1908, Weber used the concept of 'culture' rather than that of 'society', a word which, indeed, turns up only fairly late in Weber's writings. There is undoubtedly some truth in this observation. It would be wrong, however, to go so far as to say that there is a clear-cut division between an earlier period of Weber's scholarly career in which the historical approach prevails, and the later period which is devoted to sociological research and which culminates in Weber's gigantic, although incomplete major work *Economy and Society*. There is, in fact, one strand in Weber's work common to both periods, namely the attempt to develop sets of ideal-typical concepts which are:

> (a) applicable to social reality whether of the present or of the past and (b) useful in explaining any particular given social actions not only in the light of what these actions meant to the respective individuals directly concerned, but also from the point of view of anybody who cares for a rational orientation related to a given set of fundamental convictions and values. This could be achieved, in Weber's opinion, by a comparative analysis of social and cultural phenomena throughout past human history with particular attention given to their respective cultural significance for modern western society.[8]

It was Weber's most ambitious scholarly aim to do this in such a way as not to descend to putting forward just another set of value judgements in however veiled a form. On the contrary, he worked hard to develop systems of concepts of such a universal scope as to be consistent with even the most diverse value attitudes. This did not mean, however, that all values were simply omitted; on the contrary, the systems of conceptualizations he set out to develop should enable the individual to make the right choices in view of his own ultimate values. Without doubt Weber's point of perspective was very much one of an individualistic liberal who observed with some despair that the process of rationalization and bureaucratization seemed irreversible, and that it was likely to put in jeopardy the very sort of individualistic life which he believed to be the core of the Western tradition.

With respect to this attitude of cultural despair – to put it perhaps a little too bluntly – Weber's early studies of Roman antiquity are of far more than tangential relevance. His views about the development of modern industrial societies were formed to no small extent against the background of the social system of the late Roman Empire, which, due, amongst other things, to an economic organization depending on slave labour and political booty capitalism, was eventually suffocated by a network of monopolies, workshops run by the state, and bureaucratic institutions of various sorts. Weber's studies of Roman agrarian and social history were already concentrated on topics which remain central to all his work. He asked why, under the social and cultural conditions of the late Roman Empire, there did not and could not develop a dynamic capitalism. Weber tried to find an answer to this question by means of a comparative analysis undertaken on a truly universal scale, and he made good use of his rare ability to introduce new concepts of universal applicability in a way which seemed quite hair-raising to the professional historians of the time. Even so, Weber's studies on *Die römische Agrargeschichte in ihrer Bedeutung für das Staats- und Privatrecht*, and in particular *Die Agrarverhältnisse im Altertum*, may be described, quoting Andrewski, as 'truly structural history which shows how economic changes influenced religion, how the innovations in tactics brought about the transformations in social stratification, how the distribution of political power impeded the growth of capitalism, and so on'.[9]

What was Weber actually looking for when he embarked upon this kind of research? He explicitly stated that the main purpose of these studies was to describe the distinctive character (*Eigenart*), or rather the 'uniqueness' (*Einzigartigkeit*), of the culture of late antiquity as compared with our own. Thus, our understanding of our own culture would be greatly intensified, though perhaps only indirectly. This approach would seem to be very much in line with the methodological creed of German historicism. Yet Weber was actually aiming at something far beyond the horizons of the historical profession in his time. His comparative approach implied the development, for instance, of more and more generalized concepts which were so designed eventually to be applicable to a present-day context as well – something which was utterly foreign to the minds and conventions of orthodox historicists. Much more important, however, was that Weber's understanding of the 'uniqueness' of historical phenomena had little in common with the attitude shared by German historicists from Hegel to Dilthey. It was intimately connected with what Weber used to call 'cultural significance' (*Kulturbedeutung*), a phrase which he had borrowed from Rickert, but which he used in a rather different way. The 'uniqueness' of historical objects is, according to Weber, nothing given per se, but is established only if the historical objects in question are interpreted in the light of particular 'cultural values' (*Kulturwerte*). In other words, the 'uniqueness' of historical events is identical with the relevance they have with regard to certain values or sets of values held by the observer who in fact conveys a meaning to them. It is this sort of 'value rapport' which turns historical objects into what Weber called, in the terms of Rickert's Neo-Kantian philosophy, 'historical individuals'.

This is a line of argumentation which, in Weber's own judgement, was only an application of Rickert's theory of the cultural sciences. Yet there is one important difference: Weber did not share the belief of the Neo-Kantians in the existence of any objective 'cultural values'. As a follower of Nietzsche he was firmly convinced that there was no other foundation for values than the spontaneous decision of the personality. In this respect his philosophical position may well be described as individualist decisionism, however much this term may be disliked because of its association with the work of Carl Schmitt.[10] As already mentioned, Weber denied that the historical process as such embodies any meaningful principles, be they of a teleological or any other sort. It is only by relating 'limited segments' of 'the meaningless universe of world historical events' to 'ultimate and highest values, in which the meaning of our existence is rooted' that these segments become significant for us.[11]

This radical position was bound to confront Weber with the difficult problem of how any sort of cultural science was possible which did not end up in mere subjectivism. The radical way in which from 1906 onwards Weber took up the issue of abstention from value judgements is due perhaps to the fact that his own methodological theory was apparently extremely vulnerable in this respect. Weber, however, succeeded in finding a solution, or, to put it more cautiously, he believed he had found one. Although social scientists as well as historians were supposed to point out 'the cultural significance' of the social phenomena they were dealing with, they should not indulge in value judgements themselves. Weber repeatedly emphasized that there was a vital difference between establishing value relationships and value judgements. Whereas scholars had to avoid the former, it was their prime duty to establish relationships between social phenomena on the one hand and certain sets of values on the other. For only by pointing out 'possible "evaluative" attitudes which the segment of reality in question discloses and in consequence of which it claims a more or less universal "meaning"' did they enable their readers to take a stand on this themselves.[12]

This solution, however, is not easily understood and this very fact explains to some degree why the debate on the issue of abstention from value judgements, initiated by Max Weber in the *Verein für Socialpolitik* in 1913, has gone on up to the present day, with, on the whole, rather discouraging results. Max Weber himself considered the discovery of the 'ideal type' as being the key to a solution of the tricky problem of how to abstain from value judgements while at the same time interpreting social and historical phenomena in the light of 'ultimate values' which are introduced by the scholar as a matter of personal conviction. This is substantiated by a letter which Weber wrote to Rickert in 1904:

'I am delighted that you concur with the idea of the "ideal type". I consider such a category to be necessary indeed, in order to be able to distinguish between "value judgements" and judgements by which value rapports are established. The exact wording of this category is a matter of secondary importance. I defined it in accordance with what is called in ordinary language an "ideal marginal case" or the "ideal purity" of a typical event, or an "ideal construction" et cetera, without associating any normative connotation – that it ought to be that way – with them; furthermore, I had in mind Jellinek's use of the term "ideal type", as something which is thought to be perfect on logical grounds only, yet by no means as a normative pattern.'[13]

In his famous essay '"Objectivity" in Social Science and Social Policy' Max Weber explained at length how this new 'ideal typical' method should be implemented in the social and cultural sciences. He made it abundantly clear that the 'ideal type' was meant to be exclusively an epistemological tool, and that it in no way embodied reality as such. For this very reason the construction of 'ideal types' was in principle a matter of free choice; it was determined by practical considerations only. In order to serve its purposes any 'ideal type' had to be constructed on rational lines, in a logically consistent form. Otherwise, it would be of little use for a rational scientific discipline. Yet in addition 'ideal types' had to be constructed in such a way as to give particular attention to certain aspects of the issue in question, or to use Weber's own phrase, to enhance those aspects which, with regard to the 'cultural significance' of the segment of reality to which it applied, could be said to be of particular importance. In Weber's 'ideal type' of bureaucracy, for instance, those elements which would seem to be particularly dangerous for any society of free individuals, i.e., strict discipline, strict subordinance, pure formal rationality of its operations, etc., have been given particular emphasis. It is in this operation of enhancing certain elements of an 'ideal typical' construct that the factor of 'value rapport' comes into the play.

For it is exactly those aspects of an ideal type which deserve to be enhanced which could be considered to be of particular significance in view of cultural values. It was this quality of the 'ideal type' which made it so useful for research into the cultural significance of social phenomena. Weber stated explicitly: 'The goal of ideal-typical concept-construction is always to make clearly explicit not the class or average character but rather the unique individual character of cultural phenomena.'[14]

In 1904 Weber was still very much in the camp of historical rather than systematic studies of cultural and social phenomena. Yet he strongly objected to the distinction between individualizing and systematic cultural sciences, as was suggested by Rickert, amongst others, at the time. All social sciences, whether they are historically oriented or attempting to develop general theories, have to operate both on a systematic level and from the viewpoint of certain 'ultimate values' which convey 'cultural significance' to their findings in one way or another. Weber stated explicitly that it could not possibly be the ultimate goal of any sort of social science to establish 'systems of analytical laws', however perfected these might be.[15] On the contrary, he defended the historical approach as an essential part of modern social science, on the grounds that the ultimate goal of all social research was to enhance our knowledge of 'cultural reality', and this implied, as we have already shown, the interpretation of any given set of social facts in view of particular cultural values. One should bear in mind that for Max Weber 'culture' was a concept, which was anything but an *a priori* phenomenon: '"culture" is a finite segment of the meaningless infinity of the world process, a segment on which human beings confer meaning and significance'.[16]

It is at this point that the mutual intersection of the universal historical and sociological approach in Weber's own methodology can be seen most clearly. Weber went as far as to say: 'To the extent that our discipline attempts to explain particular cultural phenomena of an economic nature by showing that they originated in unique causes, they may be economic or not, by means of a method of causal regression, it seeks historical knowledge. In so far as it traces a particular element of cultural life, namely the economic one, through the most diverse cultural contexts, it is making an historical interpretation from a specific point of view, and offering a partial picture, which paves the way for a comprehensive historical perception of culture.'[17] It would seem worthwhile to emphasize the last sentence of this quotation, for much of Weber's own scholarly work belongs in this category, especially his sociological interpretation of the world religions.

These findings would seem to corroborate the argument that Max Weber was, in the earlier stages of his intellectual development, an historian of culture rather than a sociologist. This point, however, has to be qualified considerably. First, Weber himself remained faithful throughout his life to the methodological position which he had taken up between 1903 and 1907. Although, in fact, he considerably altered his research strategies in 1913, he felt no need to retract any of the epistemological principles which he had put forward in his theoretical writings, and indeed he continued to refer to them. He always paid the utmost attention to the historical dimension of all social phenomena, for it was only in this way, in his opinion, that their cultural significance could be ascertained at all. It was not so much the goals of his scholarly work, but rather the approaches which were subjected to substantial change after 1913. Henceforth Weber analysed social phenomena, which he considered to be of the utmost significance in view of the future prospects of liberal bourgeois societies, in the light of a truly universal historical perspective, on a more elevated level and in a much more systematic manner, yet his fundamental concerns were still much the same. It may well be said that Max Weber's later work was essentially an elaborate attempt to knit a variety of 'partial pictures' of culture into a general framework of 'ideal types', in order to get as close as possible to a 'comprehensive perception of culture', on the basis of an evaluation of all available information about the various societies in the history of mankind. Secondly, one should bear in mind that Max Weber never, not even in his early theoretical essays, suggested that the social sciences should be limited to what would nowadays be called cultural-historical studies. On the contrary, from the very beginning he made it quite clear that alongside such studies which linked social phenomena to individual historical causes – that is, by using historical methods – the social sciences had, by means of a comparative analysis of various societies or various social phenomena, to formulate sets of concepts and ideal types which could then be considered to have genuinely attained a more or less general applicability. In his dispute with Eduard Meyer, Weber pointed out that historical research ought also to serve the purpose of designing 'general concepts, analogies and rules of cultural growth which are applicable to history not only of our own, but of "any" civilization'.[18]

It must be admitted, however, that in about 1905 Max Weber was still somewhat ambiguous on this point. He left the door open both for a historical sociology which set out to analyse particular social phenomena in the light of their cultural significance, and for a systematic sociology which – although based on the comparative analysis of civilizations throughout history – could eventually dispose of the factor of historical time in favour of developing theoretical conceptualizations which might be used to interpret any given segment of past or present social reality alike. In his earlier scholarly career Max Weber clearly pursued the first rather than the second alternative. His essays on *The Protestant Ethic and the Rise of Capitalism* as well as his analyses of the great world religions belong primarily to the first category, namely historical sociology. In the *Protestant Ethic* Weber attempted to trace the origins of modern industrial capitalism. He saw the cultural significance of capitalism primarily to be that mature capitalism could do without the values and patterns of social conduct which had been the necessary prerequisites for its own emergence. Capitalism and rationalization were, in Weber's opinion, to no small extent the product of a *unique* historical phenomenon, namely the 'inner-worldly asceticism' of the Puritan sects. He embarked upon the study of the other great world religions primarily in order to corroborate his findings *ex negativo*. In the end Max Weber was convinced he had found an exhaustive answer to the universal historians' question why 'modern capitalism', 'modern science', the 'bourgeoisie' as a social class with its own peculiar ideological outlook, the rational organization of the political order by means of the modern administrative state, a 'rational law', and, last but not least, a 'rational type of music', had been developed only in the West. The *Vorbemerkung* to Weber's essays on the sociology of world religions can well be called a (however brief) substantive outline of universal history.[19]

Until 1913 the universal-historical and the sociological approaches in Weber's scholarly work cannot easily be separated; they are closely inter-related throughout. This is true particularly with regard to Weber's socio-logical study *The City* which, incidentally, would seem to be the earliest section of *Economy and Society*; it was written presumably around 1911. It may be said to be the most advanced example of the application of the 'ideal type' method to an historical object to be found in Weber's writ-ings. Here Weber presents a systematic outline of the almost inexhaustible varieties of urban cultures throughout history, which is impressive both for its universality as well as for its precision of detail. Yet it would be misleading to call *The City* an empirical study, whatever that term is sup-posed to mean. For the yardstick of 'cultural significance' can be clearly perceived, although this requires a somewhat closer inspection of the pat-terns of conceptualization used by Weber in that context. It is the rise of the politically active bourgeoisie in the commercial cities of medieval Europe which he pays most attention to and around which his whole line of argument is arranged. According to Weber, it was of the utmost signifi-cance that the artisans and traders of the cities of Medieval Europe beyond the Alps abandoned all sorts of booty – capitalism which seeks economic gain by means of extra profits due to political exploitation or monopolistic practices and, instead, embarked upon the rational pursuit of economic activities which promised comparatively small, but steady economic re-turns. Thus, they created the essential preconditions for the eventual rise of modern industrialism, just as their rebellion against the traditional po-litical authorities laid the foundations for the eventual development of the modern democratic state.

By 1913, however, an important change in Weber's methodological approach can be observed. Suddenly the 'ideal type' ceased to be exclu-sively a methodological instrument of sociological research; it became a goal of research in itself. Weber now became increasingly interested in developing sophisticated systems of ideal types as such, irrespective of the contexts in which they were to be applied to empirical reality. The point of departure is marked by Weber's essay 'Über einige Kategorien der "verstehenden" Soziologie' which was published in 1913.[20] In this essay, to which a sequel, which was never written, was intended, the construc-tion of 'ideal types' and the development of meaningful theories of social conduct is considered a primary goal, and socio-historical analysis retreats into the background, or rather, deteriorates into a mere commentary. Weber here points out the basic dichotomy of *Gemeinschaftshandeln* and

Gesellschaftshandeln. The former implies that the individuals concerned act in accordance with certain value-oriented principles often of a subjective or emotional nature which, however, have been agreed upon by more or less all of them. *Gesellschaftshandeln*, on the other hand, is defined as a form of social interaction which is based on a system of purely goal-oriented rules (*zweckrationale Regeln*), and in which no attention whatever is given to the individual motives of the acting persons involved.

Here, it would seem, Max Weber eventually establishes himself as a sociologist in the full sense. Yet this turns out to be an overhasty conclusion. For a close scrutiny shows that this conceptualization of a seemingly value-neutral quality, rests on certain fundamental assumptions about the future course of world history, which, although formulated only in a hypothetical form, have yet to be taken into account. The dichotomy between *Gemeinschaftshandeln* and *Gesellschaftshandeln* derives its 'significance' (the qualifying epithet 'cultural' may well be omitted from now on) from the assumption that there is one over-all trend in history, namely the steady advance of the type of *Gesellschaftshandeln*, at the expense of the various types of *Einverständnishandeln*, or, in more straightforward terms, the irresistible advance of bureaucratic forms of social interaction on all levels of social life: 'Admittedly the course of (historical) events leads in many individual cases also from concrete rational instrumentally oriented systems to the establishment of systems in which social action based on mutual agreements is the dominating factor. Yet on the whole, on the basis of our knowledge about the whole of past history, we observe if not always a complete replacement of social action based on mutual agreement by socially regulated forms of action (*Vergesellschaftung*) but at any rate a steady advance of instrumentally rational regulation of actions based on mutual agreement, and in particular a progressive turnover of (voluntary) associations into institutions organized on an instrumentally rational (*zweckrational*) basis.'[21] This is in fact substantially a historical statement, however formalized it may be. Weber's perspective of universal history, although it is not made explicit in this context at all, is always in evidence. His views about the future of Western societies which might develop into a new 'iron cage of serfdom' in which all forms of individually oriented social conduct are likely to be eliminated and which will be dominated by a new type of human being – namely the fully adjusted *Fachmensch* – served as a frame of reference with regard to the significance of these sociological conceptualizations, although, as such, they were kept in the background.

This is also true to a large extent for Weber's major work, *Economy and Society*, or to be precise, for the later sections of it. It is obvious, however, that Weber tried to do his best to push the historical aspect more and more into the background, and to design a universal systematization of 'ideal types' of various forms of social action in which historical time no longer plays a significant role. This trend becomes obvious, once the different sections of *Economy and Society* are distinguished with regard to the respective dates of their composition. *Economy and Society* is, as it were, not only a *torso*, but rather a mixture of several *torsos*, and, if Max Weber had had his way only the latest version would have gone to the printers, a fact to which the available editions unfortunately do not pay sufficient attention. There are at least three different layers in *Economy and Society* which overlap with one another to a considerable degree.[22] This can be demonstrated most strikingly in the case of the theory of the 'three pure types of legitimate domination' of which no less than three different versions can be found. The oldest one would seem to be 'Herrschaft durch Organisation – Geltungsgründe der Herrschaft',[23] together with the lengthy explication of the principles put forward in the following sections on 'Bureaucratic Domination', 'Patriarchal Domination' and its various historical versions, and eventually the section on 'Charismatic Domination'.[24] The essay 'Die drei reinen Typen der legitimen Herrschaft' which was published as a separate item in 1922 for the first time, is more difficult to date, yet in deviation from Winckelmann, I think it must be placed, if only for stylistic reasons, fairly late, possibly around 1918.[25] The most mature, and in Weber's view definitive version is, of course, 'The Types of Domination'.[26] If these three versions are compared, it becomes obvious that they are different both in style as well and in the degree of stringency with which the types are defined. The earliest version contains an enormous amount of historical material, and moreover it still displays some traits of the assumption that there is a specific trend in historical reality, namely the development from charismatic to traditional and, finally, to bureaucratic types of domination. In the later versions, however, Weber took pains to eliminate everything which might suggest to his readers that this tripartite typology was a reflection of the actual historical process. It is even more important in this respect that in the later versions all allusions to historical examples were being separated more and more rigidly from the main line of the argument. In the final version the historical material is used exclusively for the purpose of illustration. To put it another way, there is a definite swing away from an interpretation of social reality referring to specific historical forms of social conduct, towards a much more generalized interpretation which attempts to outline possible patterns of social conduct of individuals or groups of individuals found in the most diverse historical contexts.

In one of the later passages of *Economy and Society* Max Weber explicitly pointed out that his great undertaking of developing a universal conceptual framework for the interpretation of social reality was substantially different from any historical approach – something which could not be said for some of his earlier works. Sociology no longer had to interpret social phenomena in terms of 'cultural significance' in quite the way he had outlined a decade earlier in his theoretical writings. Weber stated explicitly: 'Sociology seems to formulate . . . type concepts and generalized rules of social processes [*Geschehen*],[27] whereas history is oriented to the causal analysis and adequate explanation of individual actions, structures and personalities possessing cultural significance.'[28] Yet it would be misleading to take this as the whole story. For Weber went on to say: 'The empirical facts which are used by sociology in a paradigmatic manner, in order to develop its own concepts, are largely, though by no means exclusively, identical with the concrete processes of action which are relevant from the viewpoint of the historian. The formulation of sociological concepts and the search for sociological rules is being undertaken in particular, although not exclusively, in view of whether they may be of any help in establishing causal relationships of a historical nature as regards social phenomena that would seem to carry cultural significance.'[29] The second part of this statement especially deserves attention in our present context, for it indicates that when he embarked on the formulation of his universalist systematization of 'ideal types' of social action, Weber had more in mind than a mere value-neutral description of empirical reality. Max Weber's impressive casuistry of 'ideal types' deliberately disposed of all material historical contents; yet nonetheless its essential promises bear the imprint of his personal perspective of universal history. Although Weber had certainly reached an altogether new level in his methodological approach to social phenomena, he nonetheless aimed at designing concepts suitable for the perception of those perspectives of the universal historical process, which could be said to be of cultural significance, at least for human beings brought up in the Western tradition. For this reason, it is somewhat dangerous to pick useful sociological concepts at random from Weber's *Interpretive Sociology* without giving much thought to the context in which they are being put forward. It is most unfortunate that Weber has sometimes become little more than a useful quarry for concepts, and ideal types. There can, in fact, be little doubt that his ideal-typical systematization of universal history was influenced considerably by a series of fundamental assumptions about the future of Western societies and the role assigned to intellectual human beings who are devoted to certain ultimate values in the emerging social systems dominated by instrumentally rational types of social interaction and gigantic bureaucracies.

This is borne out by the manner in which Weber phrased some of his key concepts, for instance the 'ideal type' of bureaucracy. The 'ideal type' of bureaucracy was deliberately designed by Weber in such a way as to underline those elements which he considered particularly relevant in regard to the future destinies of the individualistic, liberal societies of the West. It is small wonder that some sociologists found that Weber's concept of bureaucracy – in so far as it overemphasizes the role of subordinance, discipline and formal rationality – does not altogether fit the empirical reality of present-day bureaucracies. It may well be said, however, that this was intentional, that is to say that the 'ideal type' of 'bureaucracy' was deliberately designed by Weber in such a way as to serve as a yardstick which could be used to ascertain in exact terms the tremendous cultural significance which the rise of modern bureaucracies possesses for conscientious citizens living in liberal societies of the western type, and in a wider sense also for those living in other types of societies. If all this is taken into account, it would be somewhat misleading to criticize Weber's 'ideal type' of 'bureaucracy' as a one-sided concept. For it was deliberately 'one-sided', in order to serve as an epistemological tool for cognition on a truly universal-historical level.

Much the same could well be said with regard to Max Weber's theory of authority. It is derived from the assumption that there is a fundamental dichotomy between qualified, that is, charismatic leadership on the one hand, and the unreflected, disciplined submissiveness of the governed on the other. One of Weber's main concerns was how real leadership can be provided for in modern bureaucratic political systems. For this very reason he considered the form of selection of the leading personnel to be of fundamental importance for a classification of various types of domination.

Weber's concern about the dehumanizing trends in western industrial societies is clearly reflected in his *Interpretive Sociology*, especially in its later sections. It may well be said that in the ultimate analysis, *Economy and Society* is concerned with one central theme – namely the never-ending struggle of charisma as a particularly powerful social force, which Weber more or less identified with individual creative activity, on the one hand, and the routinizing forces of bureaucratization and rationalization on the other. Routinization and rationalization embody a trend towards the emergence of rigid and ultimately ossified social structures that are dominated by purely instrumentally oriented forms of social interaction. In Weber's view routinization and rationalization pave the way for the eventual rise of a new human species – namely the fully adjusted men of a bureaucratic age who no longer strive for goals which lie beyond their intellectual horizon, which is in any case likely to be exclusively defined by their most immediate material needs. Charismatic leadership, on the other hand, is capable of checking these trends, at least up to a point, and he therefore became increasingly interested in this type of socially creative action.[30] This is not to say, however, that Weber advocated charismatic breakthroughs and revolutions as the only way out of the troubles which beset modern bureaucratic societies. He maintained that under modern conditions charismatic leadership can only achieve something of lasting importance if the new impulses it generates are implemented through rational types of social organization rather than through mere ephemeral retines. To put it another way, creative charisma and rationalization must join forces, if anything of a lasting nature is to be achieved, despite the fact that, in their pure form, the social forces of 'charisma' and 'rationalization' are eternal rivals. The rise of personalities with charismatic leadership qualities is likely to have an impact on the social structures only if they can convince their 'retinue' to rationalize their own social conduct systematically according to the ultimate values which are 'revealed' by the respective charismatic messages.

The fundamental intention of Max Weber's monumental 'ideal-typical' theory of social action can be summed up in the following way:

The 'ideal-typical' constructions were supposed to serve as yardsticks which enable the scholar first to assess correctly the conditions under which individual creative action of a sizeable magnitude can occur, in past as well as present societies and possibly also in future societies – secondly, to point out their respective cultural significance. This is particularly the case with regard to Weber's 'ideal-typical' classification of 'social conduct'[31] on the one hand, and the 'Three Pure Types of Legitimate Domination' on the other.[32] It is significant that Max Weber was not satisfied with merely extrapolating trends which point to the eventual emergence of social structures which are dominated by purely instrumentally oriented forms of social conduct and formally legal bureaucratic rule. His impressive systematization of 'ideal-typical' concepts was designed in such a way as to enable his readers to discover for themselves the cultural significance of given social phenomena in view of their own highest values and ultimate goals. Weber's own personal convictions as to the future of Western societies, which he judged from the grandiose perspective of more than three thousand years of past human history, become apparent only indirectly, as the result of a painstaking interpretation.

This analysis may be rounded off by pointing out that it would give a new stimulus to sociology and history alike if we were to rediscover the depths of Weber's historical sociology more fully, since it was a hitherto unsurpassed attempt to interpret social reality in the light of meaningful assumptions about the past, as well as the future, of mankind rather than a mere description empirical reality in an extremely sophisticated terminology.

Notes

1. It is only since 1968 that a complete English version of Weber's major work *Wirtschaft und Gesellschaft* (henceforth referred to as *WuG*) edited by Guenther Roth and Claus Wittich has been available. This is a great achievement, although it is a matter of dispute whether the

translation always renders the meaning of the Weberian text in the best possible way. *Economy and Society: An Outline of Interpretive Sociology*, 3 Vols., New York, 1968 (henceforth referred to as *EaS*).

2. Talcott Parsons, *The Structure of Social Action*, Vol. 2, 2 ed., repr. New York, 1968; Reinhard Bendix, *Max Weber, An Intellectual Portrait*, 2 ed., London, 1962.

3. *Gesammelte Aufsätze zur Wissenschaftslehre*, 3 ed., Tübingen, 1968 (henceforth referred to as *WL*), p. 154, author's trans. Cf. *The Methodology of the Social Sciences*. Max Weber, trans. and ed. by Edward A. Shils and Henry A. Finch, New York, 1949, p. 57 (henceforth referred to as Shils).

4. For a more detailed elaboration on this point, see Wolfgang J. Mommsen, 'Universalgeschichtliches and politisches Denken bei Max Weber', *Historische Zeitschrift*, Vol. 201, 1965, p. 557ff., now also in Dirk Käsler (ed.), *Max Weber, Sein Werk und seine Wirkung*, Munich, 1962 (henceforth referred to as Mommsen, *Universalgeschichtliches Denken*). An earlier version of this essay 'Max Weber's Political Sociology and his Philosophy of World History', was published in: *International Social Science Journal*, Vol. 17, 1965. Extracts from this essay are published in Dennis Wrong (ed.), *Makers of Modern Social Science: Max Weber*, Englewood Cliffs, N.J., 1970.

5. Cf. Ernst Troeltsch, *Die Probleme des Historismus, Gesammelte Schriften*, Vol. 3, 1928, p. 189.

6. Emerich Francis, 'Kultur und Gesellschaft in der Soziologie Max Webers', in *Max Weber. Gedächtnisschrift der Ludwig-MaximiliansUniversität München zur 100. Wiederkehr seines Geburtstages 1964*, eds, Karl Engisch, Bernhard Pfister and Johannes Winckelmann, Berlin, 1966, p. 90ff. John Rex, 'Typology and Objectivity: a Comment on Weber's four Sociological Methods', in: Arnn Sahay (ed.), *Max Weber and Modern Sociology*, London, 1971, p. 18ff.

7. Carlo Antoni, *From History to Sociology: The Transition in German Historical Thinking*, Detroit, 1959.

8. W. G. Runciman argues in his most recent book *A Critique of Max Weber's Philosophy of Social Science*, Cambridge U.P., 1972, p. 12, that Weber 'did distinguish sociology – a term which in general he disliked – from history on the grounds that the historian does not try to construct "type concepts" or formulate "general rules" whereas the sociologist does'. This is misleading: the difference being not one of substance, but of emphasis. Weber, in fact, points out that the historian is bound to work with ideal-typical constructions; his approach differs from that of the sociologist only in so far as he attempts to demonstrate the cultural significance of such ideal-typical concepts by relating them to a sequence of 'adequate causations' of past history. See on this point W. J. Mommsen, 'Max Weber', in: *Deutsche Historiker*, ed. Hans-Ulrich Wehler, Göttingen, 1972, Vol. III, p. 71ff. where the role of historiographical methods in Weber's writings is discussed from the historian's point of view.

9. S. Andrewski, 'Method and Substantive Theory in Max Weber', *British Journal of Sociology*, Vol. 15, 1964, p. 6.

10. The interpretation of Max Weber as a decisionist thinker is also held by Jürgen Habermas; see his contribution to the debate in Heidelberg 1964, in *Max Weber und die Soziologie heute, Verhandlungen des 15. Deutschen Soziologentages vom 28. bis 30. April 1964 in Heidelberg*, ed. Stammer (henceforth referred to as Stammer), Tübingen, 1965, p. 79: 'Weber's philosophische Antwort heisst: dezisionistische Selbstbehauptung inmitten einer rationalisierten Welt' (c.f. the English ed. *Max Weber and the Sociology Today*, Oxford, 1971, p. 64). See further Jürgen Habermas, 'Verwissenschaftliche Politik und öffentliche Meinung', in: *Technik und Wissenschaft als 'Ideologie'*, Frankfurt, 1968, p. 121f. Recently this interpretation has been challenged, although, in the present author's opinion, with limited success, by Wolfgang Schluchter, *Wertfreiheit und Verantwortungsethik: Zum Verhältnis von Wissenschaft und Politik bei Max Weber*, Tübingen, 1971. Schluchter admits, however, that Weber was a 'fundamentalist', in so far as he assumed the existence of certain fundamental value-attitudes which are *a priori* to all scientific analysis.

11. *WL*, pp. 180, 213 (author's trans.; cf., however, Shils, pp. 81, 111).

12. *WL*, p. 253 (Shils, p. 151).

13. Letter of 14 June 1904, Weber papers, Deutsches Zentralarchiv II, Merseburg, Rep. 92. The relevant section of this very important letter runs as follows: 'Ihre Zustimmung zu dem Gedanken des "Idealtypus" erfreut mich sehr. In der That halte ich eine ähnliche Kategorie für notwendig, um "werthendes" und "werthbeziehendes" Urteil scheiden zu können. Wie man sie nennt ist ja Nebensache. Ich nannte sie so, wie der Sprachgebrauch von "idealem Grenzfall", "idealer Reinheit" eines typischen Vorgangs, "idealer Construktion" etc. spricht, *ohne* damit ein Sein-Sollendes zu meinen, ferner wie das, was *Jellinek* (Allgemeine Staatslehre) "Idealtypus" nennt, als nur im *logischen* Sinn perfekt gedacht ist, nicht als *Vorbild*. Im Übrigen muss der Begriff weiter geklärt werden, er enthält manches bei meiner Darstellung noch unausgeschiedenes Problem – Ich werde demnächst einmal (im Winter) die Bedeutung der Kategorie der "objektiven Möglichkeit" für das historische Urteil und den Entwicklungsbegriff zu analysieren suchen. Vorerst kommt ja durch St. Louis ein grosser Hiatus hinein. Auch schwankt mein Befinden konstant, so dass ich zu meiner Hauptarbeit Protestantische Ethik und Geist des Kapitalismus nur sporadisch komme.'
14. *WL*, p. 202 (Shils, p. 101).
15. *WL*, p. 175 (Shils, p. 76).
16. *WL*, p. 180 (Shils, p. 81).
17. *WL*, pp. 163f. Trans. by Shils, p. 66, modified by the author.
18. *WL*, p. 265.
19. *Gesammelte Aufsätze zur Religionssoziologie* (henceforth referred to as *RS*), Vol. 1, Tübingen, 1920, pp. 1ff.
20. *WL*, pp. 427ff. This important essay has not yet been translated into English.
21. Ibid., pp. 470f.
22. These three layers in *Economy and Society* are substantially different both with regard to the style of presentation, and the substantive intentions which Weber had in mind when he wrote them. The approximate dates of their composition are as follows:

composed about

1911–13	1. 'Die nichtlegitime Herrschaft: Typologie der Stadt', *WuG*, Vol. 2, pp. 735–822.
	Die Wirtschaft und die gesellschaftlichen Ordnungen und Mächte', *WuG*, Vol. 1, pp. 181–244. 'Politische Gemeinschaften', *WuG*, Vol. 2, pp. 514–40.
	'Soziologie der Herrschaft ', with the exception of the 'Drei Reinen Typen der legitimen Herrschaft', *WuG*, Vol. 2, pp. 541–50, 559–734.
1913–14, 1916	2. 'Typen religiöser Vergemeinschaftung (Religionssoziologie)', *WuG*, Vol. 1, pp. 245–381.
about 1918, 1919–20	3. 'Die drei reinen Typen der legitimen Herrschaft', *WuG*, Vol. 2, pp. 551–8.
	'Soziologische Kategorienlehre', *WuG*, Vol. 1, pp. 1–180.

Roth and Wittich paid considerable attention to this problem and in this respect their edition is better than the original German one. It is to be hoped that the forthcoming 5th German edition will bring a substantial improvement.
23. *WuG*, Vol. 2, 547f.
24. *WuG*, Vol. 2, pp. 541–50, 559–95.
25. *WuG*, Vol. 2, pp. 551–8. Roth and Wittich were well advised not to include this section in the English ed., as it forms a rather erratic block in the 4th ed. of *Wirtschaft und Gesellschaft*.
26. *WuG*, Vol. 1, pp. 122–76.
27. Roth renders the term *Geschehen* as 'empirical process' which to the present author seems a characteristic distortion due to the particular viewpoint of a predominantly empirical social scientist.

28. *WuG*, Vol. 1, p. 9; cf. the version of Roth in *EaS*, Vol. 1, p. 19.
29. Ibid.
30. Cf. below, pp. 79ff.
31. *WuG*, Vol. 1, p. 11ff. (*EaS*, Vol. 1, p. 22ff.)
32. *WuG*, Vol. 1, p. 122ff. (*EaS*, Vol. 1, p. 212ff.)

CHAPTER 2

The Champion of Nationalist Power Politics and Imperialism

Max Weber can be said to have been with some qualifications one of the few German liberals who were staunch supporters of parliamentary democracy in Germany long before the First World War. His violent criticism of the 'personal rule' of Wilhelm II and his bombastic and pretentious speeches which had helped so much to create an utterly negative image of Germany in the western world, was well known, and hence his points seemed to have been well taken. His forceful attacks on the Bismarckian Constitution and its shortcomings, which were published in a series of widely read newspaper articles in the influential *Frankfurter Zeitung*, were still in the minds of those who could remember the years of the First World War, all the more so as Weber's advocacy of an immediate reform of the constitution in June 1917 had given a particular boost to the reform movement. Weber's passionate attempts to convince the German bourgeoisie in 1918–1919 that their duty was to join forces with the Social Democrats in a common endeavour to restore order and to establish a parliamentary democracy, had also made a lasting impact on public opinion. His eloquent campaign for a president directly elected by the people even found realization in the Weimar Constitution. Although this was in fact due to a variety of coinciding factors – above all the fear of the bourgeoisie parties that an all-powerful parliament would be a dangerous weapon in the hands of the Socialists – a great many people gave Weber the credit for the introduction of a popular presidency, thereby overrating the role he actually played. All these instances became part of the image of Max Weber, as it emerged after his sudden death on 14th June 1920.

Among the 'Weber circle' around Marianne Weber (its most prominent members were Karl Jaspers, Karl Löwenstein, Melchoir Palyi, and Eduard Baumgarten who was, however, at that time still a student) there emerged the idea that Max Weber had been a potential political leader of the German nation at one of the most depressing junctures of its history, but that his services had not been accepted. In other words, that the professional politicians of the day had refused Max Weber the chance to exert the influence and to exercise the power which he as a born political and intellectual genius ought to have been given.[1] This legend circulated particularly among German intellectuals, and it seems to have had a lasting influence, the more so as many people were agreed upon one point: that the failure of the Weimar Republic had been due primarily to the lack of first-rate political leaders.

In the decade after 1945, the political and intellectual climate in Germany was largely moulded by a renaissance of the political and cultural traditions of the Weimar period. Many leading politicians and intellectuals of the twenties now rose once again to major positions in German public life. The recourse to Weimar and to democratic strands in the German traditions before 1918, helped gradually to re-establish some degree of political self-confidence among the German people, after it had been utterly shaken by the fearful news of what had been done to the world, in the name of the German nation, during the reign of National Socialism. It was only too natural that in such a situation Max Weber once more came to be considered one of the 'forefathers' of German democracy. Neither Jacob Peter Mayer's *Max Weber and German Politics* – a book written during the Second World War, in which Weber was described as a 'new machiavellist' who had to bear part of the responsibility for the disastrous course of recent German history – nor Gerth's and Mills's mildly critical, liberal assessment of Max Weber's political thought were accorded much attention.[2] Against this background any critical analysis of Weber's political views and his part in Wilhelmian politics was bound to cause considerable repercussions. The older generation was satisfied to see Max Weber in the perspective which had already been built up in the twenties. His well-argued criticism of Wilhelmian Germany and Wilhelmian society seemed to them a good point of departure for a reassessment of Germany's more recent history. For the younger generation of Germans who were up to a point successfully 're-educated' after the war by the educational policy of the American and British occupation administrations along the lines of a modernized philosophy of natural rights, it was somewhat more difficult to follow this path. The disaster of National Socialism was still vividly in their minds, and this made them inspect more carefully even those ideological positions which had hitherto passed as being more or less democratic. The author's book *Max Weber und die Deutsche Politik* which was written in 1958, was clearly influenced by this intellectual climate. Even the most superficial inspection of Weber's various political writings was after all bound to reveal not only his criticism of Wilhelmian Germany and his advocacy of a parliamentary system, but also his passionate, even violent nationalism, as well as his strong emphasis on the necessity of power politics, attitudes which would seem to belong to the cherished traditions of German politics which the Germans now boasted of having overcome once and for all. Under the given conditions, however, any exposure of these features in Weber's political thought was bound to produce strong reactions, since it violated the taboo under which the recent past had been put by the older generation, after the traumatic experience of the Weimar Republic and the reign of Hitler. The discussion which developed may best be summed up in the words of Raymond Aron: 'This re-interpretation of Weberian politics caused an outrage because it robbed the new German democracy of a "founding father", a glorious ancestor, a spokesman of genius.'[3]

Initially this appeared to be more-or-less part and parcel of *les querelles allemandes*, but it soon became obvious that more was at stake. It goes without saying that it is difficult to mark a clear boundary between Weber's scholarly achievements in sociology and in political theory, and his political convictions. Max Weber, of course, did his utmost to keep politics and scholarship apart, and he took pains not to plunge into superficial 'value judgements' more or less thinly veiled in a scientific language. Yet it would be misleading, and ultimately abortive if one were to take this as a starting point for a strategy of immunization of Weber's sociological achievements, as has sometimes been suggested. There is in fact a fairly intimate connexion between Weber's scholarly work and his political creed; in a way they are even two sides of the same coin. Weber's scholarly work has certainly been substantially stimulated by political considerations of a very fundamental nature.

In view of this, it seems worth attempting an assessment of Weber's attitudes and thoughts about nationalism and imperialism. In doing so, Weber's actual role in the politics of his time, and his theoretical views on the issues of nationalism and imperialism, have to be given equal consideration.

Max Weber was brought up in an intellectual climate which largely bore the imprint of German National Liberalism. Even though Weber began to question some of the basic premises of this political creed quite early in his life, he undoubtedly took up a nationalistic attitude which was very similar to that of the bulk of the National Liberals in the 1880s and 1890s. When Weber declared it to be a first principle that the enhancement of the power and prestige of the German nation state must be the fundamental guideline of all politics, he did not differ markedly from the position of a great majority of the German middle classes. It must be realised that Weber was, as much as most of his contemporaries, subjected to the overriding influences of an age dominated by the ideology of nationalism and the prestigious idea of the nation state.

What appears to make Weber outstanding among his contemporaries is not that he was less nationalistic than others, but that he publicly propagated fairly early in his career the principle of the 'primacy of the interests of the nation state' with regard to all spheres of social and political life, refusing to make comfortable compromises even with the best of reasons or excuses. For this very reason he can in a specific sense be called a rational nationalist – in as much as he declared the national idea to be a kind of ultimate value which had to come first in politics and economics alike. Max Weber attempted to subject his whole political as well as his intellectual and scholarly activities to this principle, and he did so with the utmost rigour. This very fact perhaps explains why he at times appears to be a sort of hardheaded nationalist. In principle, at least, Max Weber adhered to 'the primacy of the interests of the nation state' to the end of his life, with a stubbornness that, at first sight, is somewhat difficult to reconcile with his scholarly findings about the nature of modern nationalism and imperialism.

It is in the context of Weber's studies of the social conditions of the farm labourers in the eastern provinces of Prussia – which he embarked upon in 1891 on behalf of the *Verein für Socialpolitik* – that the issue of nationalism enters his scholarly work for the first time.[4] The issues involved had in fact an important nationalistic dimension. Since 1884 the Germans, or at any rate the National Liberals, had shown considerable concern about what seemed to them the gradual 'Polonization' of the East Elbian provinces of Prussia – as more and more German farm labourers were migrating to the west, and in turn more and more Polish workers, mostly from Galicia, were moving in and, although this was made more difficult for them by Government regulations, they were settling down in these areas in substantial numbers. The research project which Weber joined had been launched by the *Verein für Socialpolitik* in order to find suitable legislative measures for keeping the German farm labourers on the land and hence for preventing the immigration of more Poles. Max Weber explored the problems involved thoroughly. He vividly described the fairly desperate social conditions of the farm labourers in the East Elbian areas drawing from extensive empirical material, collected by techniques of empirical research which were considered to be almost revolutionary at the time. Yet he was not content simply to draw up some legislative proposals which might help improve the living conditions of the German-born farm labourers in the respective areas. Rather, he concluded, there was no point at all in trying to improve their lot by means of social policies, since the causes of the migration of the German farm labourers to the west were much more fundamental. Weber described them as follows:

Firstly, the steady advance of capitalist methods of production in the East which resulted in the disruption of the time-honoured patriarchal ties between the landlord and his farm-hands.

Secondly, together with the former, the irrational desire of the farm labourers to be 'free'.

Thirdly, the inescapable fact that the Prussian Junkers were, for over-riding economic reasons, not in a position to raise the living conditions of the farm labourers to such a level as to put an end to the 'flight from the countryside'. Under the given conditions – that is to say, under the economic pressure of the competition of the overseas grain producers on the German market (1894 was the peak of the European agrarian crisis) the landlords were, in Weber's opinion, bound to employ cheap Polish seasonal workers rather than German labourers in order to survive eco-nomically, as the subsistence wages of Polish workers were well below of that of their more fortunate German colleagues.

In analysing these results Weber was guided by the principle of the preservation, and as far as possible, the strengthening, of the German nationality in the eastern provinces of Prussia. It goes without saying that this principle carried, in his opinion, over-riding weight. He thus arrived at conclusions which seemed all too logical, however radical they appeared to a great many people at the time. Weber suggested as practical measures: first, the closure of the Eastern frontiers of Germany to all seasonal labour as well as the prohibition of any further immigration of Polish people, and secondly, the repartitioning of the huge estates in the east, and their gradual replacement by small farms which, with regard to the labour force employed would be largely self-sufficient, and which would not produce for the market to a substantial degree. Weber pointed out that this would necessarily mean a considerable reduction of output of agrarian products. Yet, in his opinion, the German national interest did not at all require a further increase of agrarian production, but rather the preservation of the 'ethnic' landscape, as one would put it nowadays.

The political implications of these proposals were far-reaching indeed. They were based on the following line of reasoning: if one wished to pre-serve the German nation-state as an ethnically homogeneous unit – that is to say, in this specific case, to keep the Poles out – the agriculture in the east had to be organized contrary to the economic principle of maximiza-tion of productivity and output. The vested interests of the Junker nobil-ity, whose social traditions were tied up with a style of living which was possible only on huge estates in the countryside, likewise had to give way to the national interest.

This argument, namely, that all other considerations and vested inter-ests had to give way to the over-riding interest of the preservation and indeed the enhancement of the nation state, was chosen by Max Weber as the central topic of his famous 'Inaugural Lecture' at Freiburg in 1895.[5] Here he did his best to make crystal clear that the interests of the nation state ought to have absolute priority over all other considerations; not only in practical politics, but also in those scholarly disciplines which took an active part in the actual processes of legislation and political decision-making. He considered it to be merely logical that a scholarly discipline, which called itself *Volkswirtschaftspolitik* was bound to accept the interest of the nation state as the only legitimate yardstick for matters of social and economic policy or for social and welfare legislation. Weber's famous argument that science is not supposed to deduce ultimate values from its findings which might be useful for orientation in research as well as in ordinary life – and is indeed incapable of doing so – is driven home in forceful language. Yet in this context it was meant explicitly to clear the way for the unrestricted application of the principle of the 'reason of state' as an ultimate guide line for all scholarly work, at least in all those disciplines which were expected to give expert advice to politicians as well as to the public at large.

Weber's plea for this radical standpoint was couched in a language which already shocked his contemporaries. He himself was almost pleased to learn about the irritation which his 'Inaugural Lecture' had evoked in his audience. It was indeed full of phrases which display a militant nationalism, blended with Social Darwinist and to some extent even racialist notions. Weber's contention that the Poles were an inferior race, at least in so far as they stood on a considerably lower cultural level, compared with the Germans, makes somewhat strange reading nowadays, even if we make allowance for the fact that Weber attributed this more to economic and social backwardness than to any intrinsic racial qualities of the Polish people.

The core of Weber's reasoning was that social life was essentially 'a struggle of man against man', which became even more tense under the socio-economic conditions created by the emerging capitalist system. Weber vigorously argued that no one should deceive himself as to the fundamental fact that social life, and in particular the destinies of national cultures, depend largely on the use of power, in one way or another. It was, in his opinion, futile to assume that a social and political order could be devised in which recourse to force would become less and less necessary, in particular with regard to economic life: 'There is no peace in the economic struggle for survival either: only those who take this delusion of peace for reality can possibly assume that the future will bring peace and enjoyment of life to our descendants.'[6] Weber was firmly convinced that the future harboured even more intense strife between the nations of the world, on the political level as well as in the sphere of economic competition on the world markets: 'The gloomy threat of the population problem as such, to leave everything else aside, is reason enough to prevent us from holding eudemonic views, and from assuming that there might be peace and happiness on the knees of the gods, or from thinking that there might be any other way than the fierce struggle of man against man, if the necessary elbow room is to be attained.'[7]

These words remind us of the gloomy messages of Jewish prophets, who painted a black future of their own people in order to instigate them to follow the thorny path assigned to them by God. Weber warned the German people to be on their guard, even if only purely economic issues were at stake: 'Economic competition is just another sort of struggle of nations with one another, and fighting for the preservation of our own national culture is under these conditions actually not made easier, but more difficult because material interests are being invoked inside the nation herself that tend to work against her future.'[8] Weber rounded this argument off with rather cryptic remarks about the future of mankind. 'It is not peace and happiness that we shall have to hand over to our descendants, but rather the principle of eternal struggle for the survival and the higher breeding [Emporzüchtung] of our national species'.[9]

These rather harsh statements were, without doubt, somewhat influenced by the New Nationalism which had developed in the last decades of the nineteenth century, and which drew heavily from both Social Darwinism, and a somewhat refined racialist interpretation of German national culture.[10] It should be pointed out, however, that very soon afterwards Max Weber emancipated himself definitively from all sorts of racialist notions of this kind, and that he later on passionately dissociated himself from all racialist versions of nationalist thinking. Yet throughout his life he adhered to the conclusion which he had already arrived at in the late 1890s, namely that great nations are obliged to preserve their sphere of influence and their national culture, if necessary by means of force.

Max Weber was convinced that, in an age of imperialism and unrestricted international economic competition, the German nation state simply had to embark upon expansionist policies overseas. This he believed to be not only necessary but also the logical fulfilment of the political course of the German people which had been initiated by the foundation of the Reich. Weber insisted that Germany must carry on along the path entered upon in 1871, by raising herself from a European to a World Power: 'We ought to realize that the unification of Germany was little else than a piece of folly which was committed by the nation in her old days, and which, in view of its costly nature, rather ought not to have been embarked upon at all, if this was supposed to be the end and not the initial stage of Germany's striving for the status of a World Power.'[11] Weber's staunch championship of a vigorous German *Weltpolitik* was hailed with enthusiasm by his contemporaries and his message was taken up literally by a number of very influential journalists, Hans Delbrück and Friedrich Naumann prominent among them. Weber's bold move may be considered as a decisive step towards making imperialism in Germany a fashionable attitude amongst the middle classes, in particular amongst the intelligentsia.

In the late 1890s Max Weber acted on various occasions as a spokesman of a strong imperialist policy. He declared a successful expansion, among other things, to be a necessary precondition for the upkeep of the high living standards of the masses of the population. He argued that for this very reason the working classes ought to rally behind a strong expansionist policy overseas. Weber even joined the Pan-German League, and lectured at some local meetings, largely on the Polish question. He left it again when he discovered that even the 'Pan-Germans' were not willing to take a clear-cut stand against the Junker interests as regards Polish seasonal labour. In 1897 Weber also spoke up in favour of the construction of a German battle fleet: 'only people who are altogether coddled in respect to political affairs and who are naive optimists will fail to recognize that the inevitable drive to expand economically, which is common to all civilized nations organized on bourgeois lines after a transitional period of formally peaceful competition, is again approaching a point where it will be power only which decides the size of the share of the individual nations concerned in the economic control of the globe, this being identical with the margin of facilities for the livelihood of their population, in particular their working classes'.[12] Weber propagated the necessity of German expansion vigorously and with stringent arguments. At the same time he stated over and over again that such a policy could only be pursued with any chance of success if it could count on the support of the nation at large. In order to achieve this he considered the first essentials to be a thoroughgoing liberalization, and at least a partial democratization of the German political system. The predominance of the Junkers in state and society alike could not, in Weber's opinion, be reconciled with an ambitious policy overseas. Nor was the bureaucratic system by which Germany was administered at the time capable of producing adequate political leaders who might succeed in rallying the nation behind such a policy. In this respect Weber referred time and again to the British example; he pointed out that in the British case a free people had succeeded in acquiring a huge Empire, and not a few indigenous peoples had succumbed voluntarily, rather than by force, to the British sway. Weber was a prominent representative of what has been called 'Liberal Imperialism', although in some respects he was rather more radical than the majority of the Liberal Imperialists in Germany at the time, both in foreign politics and in domestic affairs.

In principle Max Weber remained faithful to this position throughout his life, even in 1918, when he admitted with grief that Germany's role as a world power had 'definitely come to an end. Yet after the first years of the twentieth century Weber gradually modified his initial attitude. He became more aware of realities and took a more elastic line, not simply

advocating recourse to force as he had done in most of his youthful statements on the issue of Imperialism. Indeed, he soon became a sharp critic
of the kind of shallow nationalism which excelled in bombastic words, and
thought only in terms of power and brute force, while it was devoid of
any cultural substance. Weber for one would have none of the 'zoological
nationalism', as he put it, that was cultivated at some German universities, as well as in the Pan-German League and other societies of that kind
devoted to political agitation.[13]

This can be shown by Weber's attitude towards the Poles. He, who
had once claimed that it was only the German people who 'transformed
the Poles into human beings', now gradually came to their assistance.
He strongly criticized the 'Bill concerning political associations' (which
passed through the Reichstag in 1908 only after considerable wire-pulling
behind the scenes) in so far as it discriminated against the use of the Polish
language in political meetings. During the First World War he eventually
took a clear-cut pro-Polish line, pointing out that the German nation had
a cultural mission to fulfil in helping the Poles to re-establish their own
nation state. In 1917, he suggested that the Polish people should be given
a liberal constitution which would allow them a very high degree of autonomy although under the protection of the Central Powers.

Weber's attitude to German war aims was also far from extremist, especially if compared with the gigantic expansionist plans harboured at the
time in Germany in almost all political quarters. Weber objected outright
to the annexation of any territories in the west – a position which at the
time only a few people dared to take up in public; at best he was willing
to consider the question of whether Germany should annex some small
strips of territory because of their strategic importance. All he did hope
for was that it might be possible to create an east-central European *cordon
sanitaire* consisting of a series of largely autonomous small Slav nation
states under German hegemony, as a bulwark against Russia.

Yet it was not sheer abrogation of all expansionist ideas as such which
induced Weber to take up such a position. He maintained that a policy of wise moderation and restriction on the European continent was
a necessary prerequisite for any future German 'world politics'. Greedy
annexations of the kind supported by the bulk of German public opinion
were bound to estrange Germany permanently from almost all the other
European powers, and would make a successful foreign policy for the
foreseeable future absolutely impossible. On the other hand he held the
opinion that Germany had to be a power state, and that, to retain her
position among the World Powers she had been obliged to run the risk of
a European war: 'We had to be a power state, and had to take the risk of
this war, in order to have a voice in the decisions about the future of the
globe.'[14] It was also Germany's duty to do all in her power to fight the

war with all the means at her disposal, since her role as a world power was at stake and with it the position of the German culture in the world, and to some degree that of smaller European nations – the Swiss, the Dutch, the Swedes, for example – as well. Though Weber was much more realistic in his appraisal of Germany's prospects of winning the war than most of his German contemporaries, he clearly did not want her to give in. However, he was sincerely in favour of a negotiated peace, and although he had made it a rule for himself to keep clear of direct political entanglement, he supported the *Deutscher Nationalausschuss*, a formally independent propaganda organization which had been secretly organized by the government in the summer of 1916, in order to prepare public opinion for the impending German peace move which was eventually made on 12 December of the same year.[15] On the other hand, he strongly objected to the so-called 'July Resolution' of the German Reichstag of July 1917, for he assumed that this would only weaken Germany's war efforts, while being useless in bringing about an early peace.

From the end of 1917, Weber showed growing concern about the course of events, and the likely outcome of the war. He was particularly worried about the decision to conduct unrestricted submarine warfare which he had done so much to thwart, since the entrance of the United States into the war seemed to him to put an end to all hopes for a negotiated peace. He also took exception to the peace of Brest Litovsk by which the chances of winning the smaller Slav nations in the east over to the German side had been gambled away, and with it the chance of preparing the way for a general peace by concluding a reasonable peace in the East. He later remarked repeatedly that the German nation paid bitterly for these two gigantic acts of folly, which had amounted to 'challenging destiny'.

It is highly typical of Weber's political character that in the hour of defeat – in spite of his severe objections to the policies of Imperial Germany during the war – he nonetheless declined to join the huge wave of pacifism which swept the country, partly as a response to Wilson's 'Fourteen Points'. On the contrary, he considered it to be the duty of every honest German to behave with 'national dignity'. In fact, his own nationalist feelings attained a second peak, and he even dared defend Ludendorff who, rightly or wrongly, was universally believed to be chiefly responsible for the military as well as the political disaster which had beset Germany.

Max Weber was furious about the revolutionary movement mainly for nationalist reasons. In his view the disastrous outcome of the preliminary peace negotiations was a direct result of the revolution, for it had made a national *levée en masse* impossible, and hence it had hopelessly weakened the German negotiating position from the very start. He went so far as to charge the revolutionaries with the grave responsibility of having made Germany defenceless against the Poles in open defiance of the Government, in order to defend the East German territories if necessary by means of nationalist guerrilla warfare against foreign intruders. Weber would have nothing to do with the pacifist trends of the day. As late as spring 1920, in his famous public lecture 'Politics as a Vocation', he defended the principles of power politics against the pacifist mood of the day.[16]

It is not easy to reconcile the record of Max Weber's actual attitude to nationalism and power politics with his theoretical findings on the same issues. Remarkably, despite his passionate involvement, Weber was capable of analysing these phenomena with an unusual degree of insight, particularly if the level of scholarly information attained about these topics at the time is taken into account.

It should be noted that Weber's notion that it would be little more than sentimental folly to assume that power could ever be eliminated as an essential ingredient of politics, is to be found throughout his political and sociological writings. Not only did he contend that power is the very essence of politics, but he went so far as to define political systems primarily in terms of power relationships. To Weber, almost any social relationship is, or can be interpreted as a display of power, however indirectly this may be done. 'Power', it would seem, is one of the ultimate categories of his political sociology; 'power' can be legitimized, and possibly held in check by a system of balances; it may also be made almost invisible by a system of normative rules and regulations which would normally guarantee an order of things such that a recourse to physical force is exceptional. Yet it cannot be disposed of altogether. The liberal, and, later on, the Marxist dream, that it might be possible to replace 'the rule of man over man by the administration of things'[17] was in his opinion an altogether Utopian idea, and of doubtful value. Constant struggle or, in ordinary life, competition between men as well as between nations was a necessary prerequisite to any dynamics in society, and hence also to individual liberty. Pacifism as well as genuine Christian morality – as voiced amongst others by Tolstoy – Weber considered to be weak and feeble creeds; creeds not worthy of a self-confident personality. In this respect he sided with Machiavelli, although he by no means belittled the fundamental conflict between everyday and political ethics, as the Florentine thinker had done. It was the duty as well as the responsibility of the politician to live with this conflict, even at the expense of the peace of his own soul.

Weber never envisaged any other world than his own, which was largely characterized by the rivalry of nation states. He came to believe that states organized on any other lines than that of nationality were not likely to survive for long, as the case of Austria-Hungary seemed to indicate. He pointed out that the state was nowadays inevitably associated with the idea of the nation, and if not, it lacked adequate stability. Weber therefore assumed that, for a long time to come at least, nation states were likely to remain the quasi-natural units of political association and political struggle.

He was, however, fully aware of the fact that the term 'nation' was anything but unambiguous, and that it could mean many things to many men. After the turn of the century, he emancipated himself more and more from the somewhat racialist conception of the 'nation' which rather naively he had adhered to in his early years. He realized that ethnic homogeneity was by no means a suitable category to cope with the manifold problems connected with the national ideal; a common cultural heritage as well as conscious political decisions were much more important than ethnic factors. He occasionally pointed out that obviously racialist interpretations of nationality problems were not likely to succeed. There were all too many examples to the contrary, the most conspicuous example being the Alsatians who belonged to the German nation, both on ethnic and on linguistic grounds, but considered themselves nonetheless to be French citizens. He also noted that, although no less than four different ethnic groups lived in Switzerland, there existed a specific Swiss national idea.

On the other hand, his conviction that a common language was a factor of first-rate importance for a stable political system, was corroborated by the case of Austria-Hungary which showed many signs of gradual disintegration after 1916. Yet he now considered language less as an indication of the affiliation to a particular ethnic group, but rather as the most conspicuous element of a common cultural heritage. Within the frame of reference of a state-oriented conception of the nation, there gradually emerged an alternative concept which defined nation primarily as the embodiment of the cultural values and traditions held in common by a particular people. On the other hand, the connexion between the 'nation' and the 'nation state' as its power organization was never completely severed. Weber was convinced that no cultural community could survive for long without creating its own political organization – at least not in the case of larger nations. Conversely, however, the nation state derives its *raison d'etre* – that is to say its ideological legitimation – largely from the cultural values accepted and held in common by the respective national group.

On the basis of these observations Max Weber eventually came to believe that three major factors constitute a 'nation':

1. a common national language,
2. a common cultural heritage, and
3. a political organization which is endowed with sufficient military power and which is the carrier of a specific 'power prestige', that is to say which is believed to be capable of employing force against other states, if the need should arise, in defence of the honour of the nation.

These three factors are usually intimately connected, although with varying degrees of relative weight and importance. The factor of 'power' is by no means a mere technical element, for it confers a certain prestige or, as Weber puts it elsewhere, a certain 'pathos' on the nation as such: 'Time and again we find that the concept "nation" directs us to political power. Hence the concept seems to refer – if it refers at all to a uniform phenomenon – to a specific kind of pathos which is linked to an idea of a powerful community of people who share a common language, or religion, or common customs, or political memories; such a state may already exist or it may be desired.'[18] On the other hand, the legitimacy of the nation state is usually derived from the high esteem in which a common cultural heritage is held, and hence it is closely linked with the destinies of the 'cultural community', as well as with its values: 'The significance of a "nation" is usually anchored in the superiority, or at least the irreplaceability, of the culture values that are to be preserved and developed only through the cultivation of the peculiarity of a group.'[19] Furthermore the nation state defends, and possibly expands, the sphere which is dominated by its own cultural community, against rival national cultures, and for this very reason the nation state is considered by the educated classes in particular as a most worthy object of their endeavours.

About 1913, it did occur to Max Weber that things might well work the other way round – that is, the establishment of a powerful nation state might well do harm to a viable national culture. He noted that the German victory in 1871 had not fostered the development of art and literature in the political centre of Germany, a statement which reminds us of Nietzsche's rather harsh saying that the foundation of the German Empire amounted to 'the extirpation of the German spirit in favour of the German Empire'.[20] Yet Weber did not follow this up by inquiring whether this insight might put his belief in the nation as an ultimate value into jeopardy.

It is worth noting that to Weber the display of some degree of political power was an essential element of the nation state, even though he repeatedly pointed out that there were many nations which had no substantial 'power organization'.[21] In the case of Switzerland, he believed the renunciation of a power status even to be the very core of the idea of Swiss nationality. It might seem that the power element existed in this particular case as, in mathematical terms, a 'negative', yet nonetheless as a substantial factor. Weber distinguished between 'power states' on the one hand, and 'outwardly small nations' on the other, although he conceded that the latter also had to fulfil a specific mission in history. The small nation states, however, could only survive, according to Weber, under either the virtual shield of protection of a 'Great Power' or by enjoying relative security from aggression through the balance of power within the European state system by which the aggressive energies of the great power states were mutually kept in check. It is only in this way that the smaller nation states were able to enjoy a relative degree of political security, which was sometimes even given the form of the formal guarantee of their territorial integrity by the great powers. Weber used a similar line of reasoning whenever he set out to justify the German war effort. Germany being in an altogether different position than the smaller European nations – such as, for instance, the Swiss or the Dutch or the Norwegians – had a duty to fight the First World War in order to have a say in the decisions on 'the quality of the culture of the future'. She could not, with honour, allow the world to be divided up between the *'reglements* of Russian bureaucrats on the one hand, and the conventions of Anglo-Saxon society on the other, possibly with an infusion of Latin *raison'*.[22] Germany as a 'power state' had to live up to her responsibilities, not only in regard to the survival of her own peculiar culture but also, although somewhat more indirectly, on behalf of the cultures of the small central European nation states as well. In his opinion their existence depended to a considerable degree upon the existence of a strong German nation state in the centre of Europe.

As far as the scanty sources allow, one may well conclude that Weber envisaged a postwar political order in Europe, as well as in the world at large, in which the Great Powers would once more be the backbone of world politics. They were all expected to act as virtual protectors of those smaller nation states which were in no position to hold their own in an age of power politics and imperialism, but which had, on the other hand, to fulfil particular cultural duties. Weber's admittedly vague remarks about the outlines of a possible postwar European order would seem to indicate that he expected that the German Empire would continue to dominate central and east-central Europe largely by indirect means, in the face of a re-emerging Russia on the one hand and the rising power of the United States on the other, while abstaining from all direct annexations.

It depends on one's point of view whether this vision is described as an outright imperialist scheme, or as a rational assessment of the political potentialities of the time. Yet undoubtedly Weber's political ideas about the future political order of Europe were much more moderate than those of most of his contemporaries in Germany and to some degree even in the whole of the west. However strongly Weber felt about national issues – after having corrected his initial lapse as regards the Polish people – he never lost sight of the necessity to pay attention to the vital interests of other nations as well. His contention that a power state has obligations not only to its own population but also to other smaller nation states of common cultural parentage, shows the same viewpoint, although he did not always keep clear of what nowadays would be called a veiled or 'informal' imperialism.

This change of attitude is also reflected in the development of Weber's theoretical conception of imperialism. Until shortly before the war, no theoretical statements about the nature of modern imperialism can be found in Weber's writings.[23] There are only a few scattered passages in his political writings which allow a reconstruction of his views about Imperialism as a sociopolitical phenomenon. In his violent imperialist statements of the late 1890s Weber stressed, in particular, the economic advantages of imperialist expansion, even though he always referred in the last resort to the national interest as such. Until 1908, and perhaps a little later, Weber held a position in some respects similar to that of Marxism, although it originated with mid-nineteenth-century bourgeois national economists like John Stuart Mill and David Ricardo. Weber assumed – just as John Stuart Mill had argued two generations before and as Rosa Luxemburg was to maintain a few years later – that the dynamics of capitalism depended, at least to some degree, on the continuous opening-up of virgin territories all over the globe, by which capitalist industrialism would constantly be supplied with fresh opportunities of exploitation. Weber appears to have expected that the process of economic growth was bound to gradually slow down, at least in the long run. Hence the tendency of the major industrial states to secure for themselves an exclusive sphere of economic activity, to the detriment of all the others, by excluding all foreign competition from those spheres of influence by high tariff walls would gain considerable momentum. It is probably primarily for this reason that Weber spoke up so violently in favour of German expansionism. He contended that Germany must do everything within her power to secure territories overseas, that is to say exclusive spheres of economic activity, while this was still possible, that is to say, before the world was divided up into closed zones of economic control. Once the present period of international competition had come to an end, the dynamics of the economic system, the well-being of the masses of the population and, in the last resort, the degree of individual freedom as well would all depend to a large degree on the size of the nation's colonial dependencies. For this very reason it appeared plausible for liberal individualists such as Weber to become ardent and passionate champions of imperialism.

Around 1911 Max Weber was obviously no longer such a pessimist about the future of the capitalist system, although he still believed that imperialism, rather than peaceful international trade and free economic exchange, would have its way at least in the foreseeable future.[24] Consequently there was no longer an overwhelming economic necessity for imperialist expansion at all costs. This allowed Weber to assess on a scholarly basis the factors which may stimulate expansionist policies, by means of a comparative analysis of imperialist phenomena throughout history which foreshadowed Schumpeter's famous essay on 'The Sociology of Imperialisms'. Although Weber did not develop a formal theory of imperialism, he assembled vital elements for it. He dealt at length with the various economic factors which might encourage imperialist politics. He pointed out that booty-capitalism, which was interested in the monopolistic exploitation of economic opportunities opened up in the course of imperialist annexations, was the most important and, at the same time, most common type of economic influence on imperialism. He went on to say that the exploitation of monopolistic opportunities is always more profitable than the pursuance of ordinary industrial enterprises oriented to peaceful exchange with trading partners in other nations. Weber attributed particular importance, however, to the interests of the producers of war machinery, and armament materials; they are, in his opinion, whatever the outcome, directly interested in expansionist policies.

Weber did not think, however, that it would be possible to get rid of imperialism by abolishing capitalism altogether. On the contrary he argued that socialist systems were just as much inclined to exploit dependent territories as capitalist ones. Weber, as a matter of fact, went so far as to argue that the opportunities for monopolistic exploitation are the more numerous the more the public sector expands at the expense of the private sector of an economic system. For only the state can create monopolies, and the more it controls the economy, the more it does so. In other words: nationalization would only bring about an increase in the economic incentives for imperialists ventures, and lead to an intensification of imperialism. Hence competitive capitalism, in contrast to booty-capitalism, is implicitly exculpated from the charge of fostering imperialism, a line of reasoning that was taken up later by Schumpeter and Walt Whitman Rostow.

In fact, Weber did not believe that economic factors alone are sufficient to explain imperialist policies. To some degree he supported the traditional notion that 'power prestige' is an important factor in inducing great powers to pursue a consistent expansionist policy. This would seem to be in line with the interpretation of imperialism as a sort of intensified struggle between great powers, a conception which is essentially a transplantation of Ranke's conception of history, in which the Great Powers play the role of the prime movers in the European State System, onto imperialistic world politics. Yet Weber did not stop there. He demonstrated that this sort of 'power prestige' which, under modern conditions, was intimately associated with the complexity of emotional feelings which make up the idea of the nation, was conditioned by a variety of sociological factors. It is above all the intelligentsia which identifies itself with the idea of the nation, and which propagates it among the population at large. In doing so the intelligentsia is obviously motivated not only by idealistic convictions, but even more by massive material interests. For any expansion of the

national culture increases their chances of profitable employment, and –
what is infinitely more important – if the prestige of the national culture is
enhanced by successful imperialist policies, their own social status is likely
to be substantially elevated also.

In a wider sense the ruling classes, and in particular, the ruling elites, always gain substantially from successful imperialist operations. Max Weber
comes close to the modern concept of 'social imperialism' as a manipula-
tive strategy of ruling elites designed to defend their own privileged positions in the existing social system, and to forestall the imminent rise of the
working classes to power. He points out that successful imperialist ventures usually lead to an enhancement of political prestige and hence of the
positions of the ruling classes within the social system: 'Every successful
policy of coercing other countries as a rule – or, at any rate, initially – also
strengthens the domestic prestige and thereby the power and influence of
those classes, status groups, and parties, under whose leadership success
has been attained.'[25] It is for this very reason, according to Weber, that the
working classes are usually opposed to imperialism, although their own
economic position is usually improved by a policy of imperialist expansion, at least in comparison with the lot of their fellows in other, less successful countries.

In 1913, Max Weber assumed that the 'universal revival of "imperialist
capitalism"', which has always been the normal form in which capitalist
interests have influenced politics', and 'a revival of political drives for expansion' were again well under way.[26] It is noteworthy that in explaining
this he listed all those factors which since then have become the stock-in-
trade arguments of the various non-Marxist theories of imperialism. He
emphasized the imperialist interests of certain sectors in capitalist economies without putting the blame on the capitalist system as such. He drew
attention to the fact that the rivalries between the European Powers considerably intensified the struggle for territories and spheres of exclusive
economic influence abroad. Yet even more important was his observation
that since the prestige and the ambitions of the ruling classes were usually
enhanced, or, at any rate, stabilized, by successful imperialist ventures, this
was indeed a very powerful force behind the drive for imperialism. Last,
but not least, Weber emphasized the particular role of the intelligentsia
in promoting imperialism. For they are directly interested in any extension of the sphere of influence of their own national culture. It is to be
regretted that Weber never did assemble these most important elements
of a theory of imperialism into a coherent theory. Yet, even in this form,
the debate on the nature of modern imperialism, which has gone on since
then up to the present day, owes a great deal to his insight.

It may well be said that Weber, by rationally analysing the motives
to be found behind imperialism, erected considerable barriers against his

own imperialist passions. Yet he did not discard them. He was convinced that 'for the predictable future' everything pointed to a further growth of imperialist tendencies, and he saw no real alternative to it. Germany, in his opinion, could not afford to step aside, all the more so as a failure in the general scramble for territories and economic opportunities overseas was bound to be detrimental to the German economy. It may be pointed out, by the way, that Weber was hardly inclined to give preference on moral grounds to peaceful international exchange rather than to straightforward economic imperialism. He was in fact anything but an enthusiastic free trader. On the contrary, he stated bluntly that market-oriented trade with colonies or other dependent territories overseas was in principle not all that much different from exploitation by means of direct imperialist control. He pointed out that industrial societies normally draw most of their advantages from imperialism in form of payments and interest charges which fully comply with the rules of ordinary market-oriented capitalist business.

For Weber personally, economic considerations of this kind carried only limited weight after 1913. He supported imperialism now more and more on the grounds that without it an independent German national culture would, in the long run, stand little chance of survival in a world dominated by two or three Super Powers. His own position was very much in line with the cultural imperialism of the intelligentsia as classified in his own theory. In his opinion, imperialist struggle was the order of the day. It could not, and would not, be stopped in the foreseeable future, and hence it was futile, and even dishonourable, not to support the interests of one's own nation state. Apart from that, Max Weber intensely disliked the idea of a well-ordered world in which political struggle and economic competition would give way to a dubious system of universal peace guaranteed by the tyrannical rule of a Super Power. In this respect the fate of the Mediterranean culture was a discouraging example. In his essays on the decline of the Roman Empire he had found that by imposing a strict *pax romana* on the whole west Mediterranean culture, the Roman Empire had paved the way for its eventual ossification. Weber clearly did not like the idea that this might happen all over again.

Notes

1. Cf. Marianne Weber, *Max Weber. Ein Lebensbild*, Heidelberg, 1950. 2 ed. (henceforth referred to as *Lebensbild*), p. 694: 'Die Nation hatte keine Verwendung für ihn in einem Augenblick, wo jedermann nach Führern rief.' Karl Jaspers, *Max Weber. Politiker, Forscher, Philosoph*, München, 1958, 2 ed., pp. 32ff., deals at length with 'die verlorene Möglichkeit der Führerschaft Max Webers'. See also the obituaries by Ernst Troeltsch, Gertrud Bäumer, Gerhart von Schulze-Gävernitz, Karl Löwenstein, and others, in *Max Weber zum Gedächtnis,*

Sonderheft 7 der *Kölner Zeitschrift für Soziologie und Sozialpsychologie*, ed. René König and Johannes Winckelmann, Köln, 1963.

2. Jacob Peter Mayer, *Max Weber and German Politics. A Study in Political Sociology,* London, 1956, 2 ed., pp. 117f. H. H. Gerth and C. Wright Mills, *From Max Weber: Essays in Sociology*, London, 1970, 7 ed. (henceforth referred to as Gerth).

3. Raymond Aron, *Main Currents in Sociological Thought*, Vol. 2, New York, 1967, p. 248.

4. For the following sections see W. J. Mommsen, *Max Weber und die deutsche Politik, 1890–1920*, Tübingen, 1959 (henceforth referred to as Mommsen, *Max Weber*), pp. 23ff. Reinhard Bendix, *Max Weber, An Intellectual Portrait*, New York, 1960 (henceforth referred to as Bendix), pp. 38ff. and – although her presentation is rather erratic, containing a curious mixture of quotations from the most diverse sources – Ilse Dronberger, *The Political Thought of Max Weber. In Quest of Statesmanship*, New York, 1971, pp. 116f. A short survey of Weber's political views is given by Anthony Giddens, *Politics and Sociology in the Thought of Max Weber*, London, 1972, which irons out somewhat the tensions and contradictions in Weber's political thought.

5. Max Weber, *Gesammelte Politische Schriften*, ed. Johannes Winckelmann, 1971, 3 ed. (henceforth referred to as PS), pp. 1ff.

6. *PS*, p. 12 (author's trans.).

7. Ibid. (author's trans.).

8. *PS*, p. 14 (author's trans.).

9. Ibid. (author's trans.).

10. For the latter see Fritz Stern, *The Politics of Cultural Despair*, New York, 1961.

11. *PS*, p. 23 (author's trans.).

12. *PS*, p. 30 (author's trans.).

13. For a more detailed elaboration of this point see Mommsen, *Max Weber*, p. 75f.

14. *PS*, p. 174.

15. For Weber's activity on behalf of the *Deutsche Nationalausschuss* see Wolfgang Mommsen, in Stammer (ed.), *Max Weber and Sociology Today*, Oxford, 1971, p. 112, and, in a somewhat wider context, Dirk Stegmann, *Die Erben Bismarcks*, Köln, 1971, pp. 503ff.

16. *PS*, pp. 546ff.

17. Cf. below, p. 87.

18. *EaS*, Vol. 1, pp. 397f.

19. *EaS*, Vol. 2, p. 925.

20. *WuG*, Vol. 2, p. 530, note (*EaS*, Vol. 2, p. 926, note.)

21. Cf. *WuG*, Vol. 1, p. 244.

22. *PS*, p. 143.

23. For a more detailed exposition of Weber's imperialist views see W. J. Mommsen, *Max Weber*, pp. 76ff.

24. *WuG*, Vol. 2, p. 526 (*EaS*, Vol. 2, 919).

25. *WuG*, Vol. 2, p. 527 (trans. by the author); cf. *EaS*, Vol. 2, p. 920.

26. *WuG*, Vol. 1, p. 526 (*EaS*, Vol. 2, p. 919.)

CHAPTER 3

The Alternative to Marx
Dynamic Capitalism instead of Bureaucratic Socialism

Max Weber was – within the history of political ideas – the great bourgeois antipode of Karl Marx and, with much justification, he has been called a 'bourgeois Marx'.[1] This statement requires some qualification since there are substantial differences between these two great personalities. Unlike Karl Marx, Max Weber did not initiate a political movement with a distinctive ideological orientation, and he never tried to do so, although the persuasive powers which were at his disposal were possibly just as great as those of Marx. Although he always lived on the borderline between politics and scholarship, he nonetheless devoted his intellectual activities, despite great emotional strain, almost exclusively to a scholarly life. Yet it may well be said that, had there existed somewhat more progressive political conditions in Germany in the middle of the nineteenth century, Karl Marx also might have become a prominent professor rather than the great ideologist, – the role that made him a world-historical figure. It may further be said that Max Weber did not succeed in establishing a school of his own.[2] Those who may be considered to have been influenced deeply by his scholarly work – for instance Joseph Schumpeter, Robert Michels, Georg Lukács, Karl Jaspers, Karl Löwenstein, Paul Honigsheim,[3] or, in a somewhat more indirect way, Talcott Parsons or Hans Freyer or even Carl Schmitt – eventually took up intellectual positions that had little in common with Max Weber: they, for the most part, settled down in other camps, especially with regard to the issues of capitalism and socialism which are our main concern here.

Nevertheless, the intellectual influence of Max Weber on Western neo-capitalism was by no means a small affair. Such figures as Friedrich Hajek,

Hannah Arendt or Karl Joachim Friedrich, who strongly influenced Western political thought in the 1950s, derived much of their intellectual weaponry in their disputes with communism from Max Weber's arguments. This is even more the case with regard to Alfred Müller-Armack, the intellectual creator and theoretician of Ludwig Erhard's *Soziale Markt-wirtschaft* which brought about the economic recovery of West Germany with unexpected speed. The enormous revival of interest in Max Weber after the Second World War, especially because he was considered a champion of empirical social science not only in Germany but in particular in the United States must be at least partially attributed to the fact that his theories were, in principle, in line with the social and economic conditions of the capitalist societies of the west.

Any analysis of the relationship of Max Weber and Karl Marx, or perhaps more precisely of Max Weber's attitude towards Karl Marx, is faced with one initial difficulty: Weber never dealt with Marx's theories in a systematic, let alone in a comprehensive, way. We have to rely largely on casual remarks and arguments which are scattered all over Weber's political and scholarly writings. The public lecture on 'Socialism', delivered by Max Weber in Vienna in June 1918 to an audience of Austrian officers, is the only text in which the issues of Marxism and Socialism are discussed at length. Yet it cannot be considered a systematic treatment of the issues involved; nor is it scholarly, in the sense that it is free from arguments chosen for specific political as well as tactical considerations.[4]

The various, sometimes rather casual, occasionally even cryptic, remarks on Marxism which are to be found in Weber's writings do not help very much. Attempts to put them together carefully lead to rather unsatisfactory results;[5] one thing, however, can be safely concluded, namely that Weber does not appear to have read Marx and Engels widely in his early career; at least up to 1906 Max Weber referred to Marxism in the vulgar versions of the day rather than to the original writings of Marx and Engels themselves.

Weber's refutation of Stammler's *Materialistische Geschichtsauffassung*, for instance, had little to do with a dispute about original Marxism as such. In one of his early lectures at Freiburg University which was delivered before 1898, Weber referred to Marx as a man who was conspicuous for his 'contempt of men', a phrase which indicates that Weber was familiar at least with some original writings of Marx. On the other hand, all available information seems to support the conclusion that it was only fairly late in his intellectual development that he dealt with Marx systematically. Marx's *Capital* is quoted only in *Economy and Society*, whereas in the earlier writings references to Marx are generally made in a sweeping style that would suggest that Weber's knowledge of Marx at that time was largely derived from secondary sources; in particular, it may be assumed, Karl Sombart's *Der Moderne Kapitalismus*, and Heinrich Herkner's *Arbeiterfrage*.

Max Weber speaks up most strongly against Marx in his methodological writings. As has already been pointed out in a different context, Max Weber objected in principle to all 'material' philosophies of history, or in other words, to all constructions of the historical process that claim to have extrapolated either a set of objective laws or, at any rate, to have discovered an intrinsic meaning in history.[6] From his neo-Kantian point of view, which was blended to no small degree with Nietzsche, all objective schemes of the historical process, the so-called 'historical materialism' included, were completely unacceptable. The Marxist theory of history which saw the essence of the process of social change in a sequence of distinctive social formations which were defined by different forms of 'economic reproduction' and were propelled by class conflicts was, in his opinion, bare of all scientific foundation. There did not exist, according to Weber, any 'laws' in social reality; at best it was possible to construct law-like conceptualizations of social processes by means of ideal types, which could then be used as yardsticks to measure the degree to which any given segment of social reality deviated from these nomological concepts. This was the case, in Weber's opinion, not only with regard to the laws of theoretical economy but just as much with regard to Marx's conception of the dialectical process of world history, by which pre-capitalist social structures were turned into bourgeois-capitalist structures and in the end into socialist systems. One may point out that this implied a serious misunderstanding regarding the epistemological position of Marx which was, in fact, by no means as rigid as Weber assumed.

This attitude was a logical consequence of Weber's fundamental assumption that the historical universe as such is meaningless, and, at least from the potential point of view of any given observers, more or less chaotic. As we have seen, it is only by applying certain concepts and categories, formulated from the viewpoint of certain ultimate cultural values, onto a limited segment of reality, that it becomes intelligible to us. Weber was hence perfectly willing to accept Marx's interpretation of history, in terms of the various forms of production, as a most useful hypothesis which might help to gain important insights into the development of modern industrial society. Yet he was not prepared to accept this as the whole story. To put it another way, while Marx's theories were considered by Weber to be most valuable as a particular form of the ideal-typical construction, they were absolutely unpalatable to him as ontological propositions: 'Liberated as we are from the antiquated notion that all cultural phenomena can be *deduced* as a product or function of the constellation of material interests, we believe nevertheless that the analysis of social and cultural phenomena with special reference to their economic conditioning and ramifications was a scientific principle of creative fruitfulness and, with careful application and freedom from dogmatic restrictions, will remain such for a very long time to come. The so-called "materialistic conception of history" as a *Weltanschauung* or as a formula for the causal explanation of historical reality is to be rejected most emphatically.[7]

As has been pointed out by, among others, Jürgen Kocka, Weber interpreted Marx in this respect in a somewhat unfair and crude manner.[8] Marx's position, in fact, was not that far apart from his own, in so far as he did not intend to formulate purely abstract historical laws of a rigid quality. Marx's doctrine of a process both necessary and irreversible leading from feudalism through capitalism to socialism was intended to be a scheme of orientation that required the actual action of men to put it into practice – at one time the bourgeoisie, at other times the proletariat – and it is only the later interpretations of Marx's doctrines, by Engels and, eventually, by Kautsky and others, that turned them into a rigid mechanistic theory.

Even if this point is granted, it may well be said that Marx was infinitely more optimistic about the possibility of a theory of social reality which was essentially comprehensive, and not just one schema amongst others undertaken from a particular point of view. Marx's confidence in the possibility of a 'holistic' theory of history was due not only to the strong influence of Hegel, but was also closely connected with his conviction that 'consciousness' is always primarily, if not entirely, conditioned by objective economic conditions. Max Weber always remained extremely sceptical about the validity of this assumption. Although he was prepared to acknowledge the value of such an approach on a hypothetical basis he deeply distrusted any, and in particular this, virtually monocausal interpretation of the historical process. In contrast to Marx, Weber's own notions about the conditioning factors of 'class consciousness' or of 'status consciousness', were essentially pluralistic. He refused to ever make a definite choice as to whether economic or non-economic factors were decisive in the last resort.

Weber was, on the whole, extremely reluctant to admit the possibility of holistic interpretations of social reality and history. Nonetheless, it would be misleading to conclude that he abstained throughout his life from all attempts to arrive at comprehensive interpretations of the social process, as Kocka would have it. It is only in the earlier writings that he restricted his endeavours to the extrapolation of particular chains of causal relationships from the meaningless infinity of reality which seemed significant from specific points of view.[9] This is particularly the case, of course, with regard to the *Protestant Ethic and the Spirit of Capitalism*. Yet, from Weber's point of view, one could say that Marx had done just the same, by constructing a comprehensive scheme of history around the guiding principle of the modes of production, the only difference being that Marx claimed that his findings were the whole truth. Weber did not believe it possible, on purely scientific grounds, to go any further than developing ideal-typical systematizations which took account of, and described the predominant trends as well as the retardatory factors at work in history, while at the same time being attentive to their sociocultural significance. Yet he meant to do this on a truly universal scale and in such a way that all available information about the development of all known civilizations throughout history would be taken into consideration. This seemed to him the only way in which the social sciences might ever arrive at universal judgements about the nature and character of particular social structures, as well as about their significance in the light of ultimate human values and beliefs of the most diverse kind. Any attempt to go any further, and to claim 'objective' truths of any kind whatever on scientific grounds, was not only bound to fail but also likely to cause infinite harm. For at this point the freedom of the individual as well as his creative spontaneity were at stake. Any such theory was apt to be detrimental to the responsibility of the autonomous individual in making his own choice between different sets of ultimate values in so far as it imputed to him the idea that there was only one future course of events to which the only sensible attitude would be to adjust willingly. In Weber's opinion, any scientific theory must come to a halt when the sphere of value decision-making was reached.

Within the framework of the conception of social science, as presented in Weber's theoretical writings, the individuals can always opt for or against predominant social trends. With the Marxist concept, however, they appeared to be reduced more or less to mere puppets whose actions were conditioned by their class-situation according to the objective laws of 'historical materialism'. At best their revolutionary action, provided that it was undertaken at the right moment, might accelerate the emergence of a new social formation.

It follows from this that, in the first instance, it was the liberal individualist in Weber which objected to the determinist implications of Marx's theory. This is not to say, however, that Max Weber took exception to all aspects of 'Historical Materialism'. It ought to be reduced to what, in his opinion, it really was: one particular approach amongst others that did not claim to be the whole truth and nothing but the truth. The Marxist theory was acceptable to him in two forms: either as a brilliant and most important hypothesis, which deserved the utmost attention of all the social sciences; or possibly, as a political ideology, which did *not* pretend to rest on any scientific foundation whatever and was designed only to propel men into revolutionary action. It is only in this latter meaning that Max Weber was prepared to accept Socialism as a doctrine worthy of serious consideration.

He showed the utmost contempt for the German Social Democrats precisely because they claimed that the objective historical process would infallibly bring about their eventual victory. He not only ridiculed such an attitude; he did not consider it worthy of a serious political movement. Socialism, as indeed any political creed, was utterly disgusting to him in as much as it presented itself in pseudo-scientific guise: For those, however, to whom Socialism was a matter of personal conviction on moral grounds – in other words, a *gesinnungsethische* position – however bleak the objective chances of its eventual success might be, Weber had considerable respect. Although he did not share their beliefs in the least, Weber entertained intimate relations with Russian revolutionary socialists in Heidelberg during the latter years of the First World War.[10]

Max Weber was most concerned with, and objected most strongly to, what is commonly called the Marxist theory of *Ueberbau*. He was not prepared to accept the argument that all social phenomena could be sufficiently explained by reference to economic causes only: 'The argument of the materialist conception of history, that "economic factors" are in any, however specified, meaning an "ultimate cause" in the causal sequence has, to my opinion, on scientific grounds had its day.'[11] At the same time, however, Weber protested against Stammler's crude attempt to refute Marx's materialistic conception of history by simply ascribing to all relevant social data in any given social framework a 'materialist' quality.[12]

Weber's objection to all monocausal interpretations of an economic nature does not necessarily mean that he took an idealist position. The *Protestant Ethic and the Spirit of Capitalism* is commonly held to prove the case for the autonomy of idealist, and specifically religious forces in history. However, it was by no means intended to be a direct refutation of Marxism, although Weber did present his thesis in 1918 in a series of lectures at the University of Munich, though not without some reluctance, under the somewhat misleading heading: 'Positive Critique of the Marxist theory of history'.[13] In fact Weber never claimed that his thesis on the origins of capitalism had definitely answered the question why and how the capitalist industrial system did emerge. He repeatedly stated that he had laid bare just one set of factors, while there were many others which must also be considered to form necessary preconditions for the rise of capitalism. Furthermore, Max Weber tended to describe capitalism in much the same way as did Marx: as a world-historical phenomenon of an irresistible quality, as one of the great revolutionary forces in the modern world. Weber, in fact, came very close to Marx's position when he argued that mature capitalism can survive without the specific mentality which was the offspring of puritan asceticism. In an almost Marxist fashion he described the modern capitalist system as an irresistible social force which coerces men to subject themselves quasi-voluntarily to its objective social conditions, regardless of whether they like them or not. Henceforth they have got to be *Berufsmenschen*, for the system of modern industrial capitalism does not permit otherwise. At this point Max Weber is, in fact, closest to Marx's contention that capitalism is substantially an inhumane form of social order. Yet Weber refused to go all the way with Marx on this point. He maintained that even under the social conditions created by modern capitalism it is not just the 'dynamics of material interests' which determines the course of events, but also the dynamics of 'ideal interests'. Both, the 'material interests', and the 'ideal interests', must be taken into account in any analysis of the historical process.[14] Max Weber took great pains to demonstrate, first in the *Protestant Ethic*, and later in his studies on the world religions that 'ideal interests' may bring about social change as well; and even further that they may well become, under particular conditions, a revolutionary force, even though – or possibly because – they have nothing at all to do with motivations of an economic nature.

It is on this point that Weber stands farthest from Marx. In contrast to Marx, he seriously believed that the individual who is oriented to and directed by ultimate values of whatever kind – and the more the latter are in contradiction to everyday reality, so much the better – may be an ultimate, irreducible force in history, in so far as he may find ways and means to reconstruct a given social context in accordance with these ultimate values. The actual results of such individual actions are, of course, largely conditioned by the specific social situation in which the individual finds himself, but the initiating steps as such cannot easily be traced back to economic or other primary motives.

Even at this point there exists a fundamental analogy between Max Weber and Karl Marx, or at any rate the author of the *Philosophical Manuscripts* of 1844. Karl Löwith has demonstrated in a masterful essay which is still among the best pieces ever written on this topic, that both thinkers were concerned with the same fundamental issues, namely the possible future of man as a human being under the conditions of the emerging industrial system.[15] Marx pointed out that under the capitalist system of production the workers had been forced into a state of complete 'alienation' or, to put it in another and more fundamental way, they have been deprived of their natural birthrights as human beings. In addition, the capitalist system of surplus value deprives them also of the value of their own work and keeps them permanently in a condition of relative social deprivation. According to Marx the capitalist system was bound to create an inhuman world since economic forces did not allow the bourgeoisie to treat the workers decently, and to pay them high wages. On the other hand, he was optimistic enough to assume that at the same time the capitalist system was producing the forces which would eventually help to destroy it and bring about a new social order in which 'alienation' would have come to an end.

Max Weber was just as concerned as Marx was with the inhuman consequences of modern industrial capitalism. Yet he did not conceive them primarily in terms of the objectively (or possibly only subjectively) depressed social condition of the working classes and of their deprivation of the means of production; rather, he had in mind the inhuman tendencies of the social institutions created by capitalism. Capitalism depended more or less on formal rationality in all spheres of social life. It was, moreover, driven by irresistible forces to create conditions which would allow a maximum of productivity and a maximum degree of efficiency. For this very reason, it was pushing all forms of individually-oriented social conduct more and more into the background. To put it in other words, the further advance of capitalism was inevitably tied up with the rise of ever more efficient bureaucracies, and an ever-greater degree of formal rational organization on all levels of social interaction. Weber envisaged that this process was likely to eventually result in the emergence of a 'new iron cage of serfdom', in which all forms of valueoriented social conduct would be suffocated by the almighty bureaucratic structures and by the tightly knit networks of formal-rational laws and regulations, against which the individual would no longer stand any chance at all.

Weber argued, in words which remind us of Marx's prophetic statements about the same subject, that the rise of Capitalism could no longer be halted. Nor did he even consider such a possibility although he was fully aware of the dangers to a human order of things associated with it. There was obviously no easy way out of this basic dilemma. Clearly, there was little reason to assume that in the course of the further development of the capitalist system things would straighten themselves out, even with such violent convulsions as those which Marx had assumed would take place. Weber could not see why the situation would be improved by a socialist revolution. It was just as futile, in his opinion, to give oneself up to a posture of mere emotional opposition to capitalism and bureaucratic social structures. One had rather to put up with the conditions of a 'disenchanted world' created by capitalism and modern rational science. Only by accepting the principles of rationalization and by applying them to his own conduct can the individual emancipate himself from the state of 'alienation' and assert himself again as a free personality – as Löwith has put it, possibly somewhat exaggerating Weber's position in this respect.[16]

Thus Weber considered Marx's suggestions on how to solve the problem of man as a human being in industrial society to be insufficient and inappropriate. For the real danger was the rise of more and more almighty bureaucracies, and not simply the private ownership of the means of production and the relative or absolute exploitation of the working classes to the advantage of their masters. He pointed out that nationalization of the means of production would not substantially alter the situation of the individual. Socialization was not likely to bring about the emancipation of the working classes from their status of 'alienation'; rather it would make it far worse. 'Any socialist economy organized on rational lines . . . would retain the expropriation of all the workers and merely bring it to completion by the expropriation of the private owners.'[17] This would simply mean another step towards further bureaucratization of the economy and, indirectly, of the social system as such. Rather than making the worker freer, Socialism would, in fact, make him even more dependent on the men who actually control the 'means of production', and besides would speed up the process of bureaucratization even more.

In 1917 many people in Germany discussed whether the state-controlled war economy would gradually lead to a Socialist system. Weber argued that this was not such an easy thing to attain as many people assumed and pointed out that nationalization of the means of production in whatever way it might be brought about would mean a further increase of bureaucratization. He put this most forcefully: 'A gradual elimination of private capitalism is no doubt theoretically possible – even though it is not such a trifling matter as many *literati*, who do not know anything about it, dream – and it will certainly not be brought about by this war. But let us for once assume that it will succeed: what would that amount to practically? Would this mean a destruction of the iron cage of modern industrial labour? No! Rather the administration of all nationalized or possibly "communalized" enterprises would then become bureaucratic as well.'[18] This in turn was bound to give a further boost to bureaucratization: 'In combination with the dead machine it [i.e. the bureaucracy] is at work to set up the iron cage of that bondage of the future to which perhaps someday men like the fellaheen in ancient Egypt will helplessly be forced to submit . . .'[19]

Weber's position may be summed up as follows. The abolition of private ownership of the means of production under the conditions of an industrial economy – regardless of whether it would be brought about by the socialist revolution and the 'dictatorship of the proletariat', or by a gradual process of evolutionary nationalization according to the revisionist model – did not substantially alter the situation in regard to the pressing problem of his own age, namely the question of how 'to save even any remnants of "individualist" freedom of action in any sense whatever' against 'the overwhelming trend towards bureaucratization'.[20] In Weber's judgement, it was 'the dictatorship of the official, rather than that of the proletariat, that was – at any rate for the time being – gaining ground constantly'.[21] Neither did he share the enthusiastic belief of many Marxists that the 'dictatorship of the proletariat' was a suitable way of paving the way for a society in which oppression of any kind would be abolished; indeed, he thought this assumption was incredibly naïve.[22]

It would be wrong, however, to draw from this the conclusion that Max Weber discarded Marx's theory altogether. As is borne out by a systematic analysis of Weber's sociological as well as his political writings, this is by no means the case. In fact he took pains to integrate all that he considered valuable in Marx's analyses of industrial society into his own sociological system. For one, he accepted in principle the concepts of 'class' and 'class struggle', and he once more came very close to Marx in acknowledging that the economic situation of a given group of persons determines their 'life chances' to a very high degree: 'It is a most elementary economic fact that the way in which the disposal of material property is distributed among a plurality of people, who are meeting competitively in the market for the purpose of the exchange of goods, in itself creates specific life chances.'[23] This is not to say that Weber accepted Marx's predominantly economic determination of 'class'. It should be noted that in a later version of *Economy and Society*, Weber developed a much more differentiated scheme of class structure than he had thought acceptable a few years before.[24] He distinguished between three types of classes, namely 'property classes' (*Besitzklassen*), 'professional classes' (*Erwerbsklassen*), and 'social classes', the last category being far less narrowly defined. This, at, first sight, rather pedantic classification is typical of Weber's line of reasoning. Weber made a distinction between 'property classes' on the one hand, and 'professional classes' on the other hand, because he thought it most important to differentiate between those class interests which were merely interested in the upkeep of the social order, and those which were directly involved in the capitalist production process, and therefore in favour of progress and change. Both the 'property classes' and the 'professional classes' were differentiated even further. Weber distinguished between 'positively privileged classes' and 'negatively privileged classes'. 'Positively privileged classes' of the former category, that is to say *rentiers* of all kinds, draw their income mainly from rents and other fixed property; 'negatively privileged' groups of the category of 'property classes', are, as a rule, ' unfree', and 'underprivileged', or even 'outlawed' as, for instance, the slaves in various economies of the ancient world; they have no chance whatever to alter their lot substantially. Weber points out that this is therefore a typically 'non-dynamic' type of class stratification in which class struggle and class revolutions are likely to have no place.[25] Blind revolts may occur but they are not likely substantially to change the existing order of things.

The concepts of 'class' and 'class struggle' apply more directly to the antagonisms within the 'professional classes'. It should be noted, however, that Weber defines the class character of the 'professional classes' – which include the entrepreneurs as well as the 'professions' *and* the workers – in a way which is very different from the Marxist one. The decisive criterion is not the ownership or the disposal of property but the actual degree of participation in the entrepreneurial management as such, and also the respective chances to defend the monopolization of the entrepreneurial positions by means of influencing the economic policies of the state or of the various organized pressure groups. Here Weber again differentiates between the 'positively privileged classes', which consist, on the one hand, of the entrepreneurs and the various professional groups with a highly specialized training – such as solicitors, scientists, doctors or artists, and even workers with special skills who cannot be replaced easily – and, on the other, of 'negatively privileged classes', that is to say the bulk of the workers. It is only the latter who have nothing else to sell on the market than their mere working capacity. This classification deserves particular attention in so far as it takes into account a specific feature of mature industrial capitalism, namely the division between the nominal owners of capital and the managerial class which in fact largely monopolizes actual decision-making. Weber seeks to justify this classification by pointing out that it is not so much the formal ownership of property, but rather the 'monopolization of entrepreneurial leadership to the advantage of the economic interests of one's own class' or, as far as the workers were concerned, their deprivation from any participation in the managerial decision-making process, which actually matters.[26]

This is a rather pedantic ideal-typical scheme, yet it enabled Weber to demonstrate that 'social classes' were anything but homogeneous entities. Even within the 'positively privileged classes', namely the propertied and educated classes, there were conflicting economic interests at work. On the one hand the interests of the 'rentiers' in economic and social and hence also in political stability, and on the other hand the entrepreneurial interest in dynamic economic growth. To some degree at least this was the case with regard to the working classes as well. The relatively small upper stratum of workers with 'monopolistic skills' was not particularly interested in substantial change in the economic and social structure. Weber was, however, somewhat ambiguous over the question whether this differentiation among the working classes was likely to become less important in the future as a consequence of the advance of automation, or whether the trend towards a further disintegration of the working classes, which was prevailing in Weber's own lifetime, was to continue. In this context Weber had been worried by much the same observation as Marx and, indeed directly referred to the last, unfinished section of *Capital*, which indicates that Marx had planned to devote particular attention to this pressing problem.[27] In view of the apparent diversity of interests, even among particular classes or sections of classes, Weber thought that Marx's class stratification according to mere ownership of property, that is to say capitalists on the one hand, and workers on the other, was insufficient, although hitherto he more or less accepted it himself. Weber therefore proceeded to put forward a much more specific model of class stratification which consisted of four social classes: namely first the working class; secondly the petit bourgeoisie; thirdly the intelligentsia so far as it did not own any substantial property, and the civil servants as well as the specially trained white-collar workers; and last, but not least, the owners of property and those groups privileged by a higher education (*Bildung*).[28]

Even with these substantial modifications of Marx's class concept, Weber did not agree with the exclusive importance Marx attached to it. He doubted whether affiliation to a particular class had really such a decisive strategic importance in market-oriented societies, as had been attributed to it by Marx. Weber argued that the actual social conduct of a particular social group is by no means always determined by its 'class situation', or its particular 'class interest'. 'Every class may be the carrier of any of the innumerable forms of class action which are possible but it will not necessarily do so'. He went on to say that there was no point in hushing up this basic truth by resorting to the concept of the 'false class-consciousness': 'The fact that men in the same class situation, as a rule, react to constellations of such vital importance as those of an economic nature in forms of mass actions that take such a direction as will suit their own average interests most . . . does not at all justify those pseudo-scientific operations with the concepts of "class" and "class interest" which are so common nowadays, and which have been classically formulated in the assertion of a gifted author that: the individual may be in error as to his interests but that the "class" is "infallible" in this respect.'[29]

The obvious reason why Weber took exception to Lukács's famous phrase was because he was firmly convinced that social actions are by no means determined by economic interests alone, not even in situations in which economic considerations are most evidently to the fore. Weber maintained that human beings by no means always act along class lines, but that they are also influenced by a great variety of non-economic factors, for instance, tradition, religious beliefs, or value attitudes of the most diverse sorts, that is to say, factors which cut right across class stratification. It is at this point that 'ideal interests' again come into play. In Weber's opinion they are just as important in determining the action of human beings as the instrumentally-oriented forms of social conduct which are imposed on the individual by the anonymous forces of what Weber occasionally called 'the lifeless machinery' of capitalist industrialism.

To sum up we may say that Weber accepted a good deal of Marx's arguments as well as some of his conclusions. He entered them in that column of the balance sheet where all those social forces were registered which were supplementing the steady advance of the process of bureaucratization and rationalization. It is noteworthy, by the way, that Weber's technique of extrapolating trends from social reality, is in a way similar to that of

Marx. Both formulated their key concepts in such a way that the imminent trends of the social process could be, after all, deduced from them, without having any further recourse to empirical data. Marx's concept of capitalism was so designed as to be necessarily self-destructive in the long run. Weber's concept of bureaucracy, on the other hand, displays an inborne, insatiable appetite for more and more formal rationalization; bureaucracy of necessity reorganizes everything it comes into contact with according to strictly 'instrumentally-rational' principles. Even Weber's ideal-typical description of modern capitalism, as the formally most rational, and hence the most efficient, form of social organization ever attained in the history of Mankind, is much closer to Marx than is usually realized.

Max Weber's 'basic sociological categories of economic action', are, in a way, his final word on the issue of Capitalism v. Socialism. In this context the dichotomy between 'market economy' (*Verkehrswirtschaft*), on the one hand and 'planned economy' (*Planwirtschaft*), on the other, is formulated as an ideal-typical tool in order to distinguish clearly between capitalism and socialism.[30] The 'market economy' is more or less identical with what is commonly called a capitalist system, whilst the 'planned economy' means a state-directed, centralized economic system which, in Weber's opinion, was the most feasible type of a socialist economy. Weber defined both types as follows: 'The satisfaction of needs through a "market economy" will be said to take place in so far as it results from forms of the fulfilment of economic demands which are made possible only on the basis of self-interest, which are oriented to exchange probabilities, and which are socially realized by the exchange of goods. The satisfaction of needs through a "planned economy" will be said to take place in all cases where the fulfilment of economic demands is regulated by substantive principles which may have been either enacted by legal procedure, or agreed upon, or imposed.'[31] Weber always held the opinion that the market is the key function of any capitalist system. In this ideal-typical definition he emphasized the role of the market even more strongly than ever before, as being the source of both the specific form of rationality of the capitalist system and of its dynamism. It is this idea that was to influence the neo-Liberalists of the 1950s so greatly.

The identification of socialism with planned economies was, however, something new. Weber was in fact himself somewhat reluctant to do so and remarked correctly that Marxist socialism was much more concerned with the forms of production than with the forms of distribution of wealth.[32] Yet under the impact of the Russian experience and the influence of the debates about possible forms of a realization of socialist ideas by further extending the wartime system of governmental control of the economy which had been practised in Germany since 1917 which Weber had followed with a mixture of disgust and interest, he considered a 'planned economy' to be the only realistic form in which the idea of socialism could be put into practice at all.

Although Weber was careful to point out that, on scientific grounds, a case could not possibly be established for either type of economic system, he, in fact, pointed out time and again that only the 'market economy' is capable of attaining a maximum degree of 'formal', or as we would say nowadays, instrumental (*technische*) rationality, particularly regarding the exact rational calculation of all economic operations. Any socialist economy, especially if it goes so far as to abandon a market-oriented system of prices, would have to cope with a substantial diminution of 'formal calculating rationality'.[33] It is almost impossible to escape the conclusion that the concept of 'formal rationality' is identical with the principle of maximization of efficiency. It may be argued that Weber himself never put it like this explicitly. However, on numerous occasions he strongly emphasized that capitalism is infinitely superior to all other known forms of economic organization precisely because it alone is capable of organizing all its activities on a purely formally rational basis. If the criterion of maximum efficiency is taken as a yardstick in order to evaluate the 'market economy' on the one hand, and the 'planned economy' on the other, the prize goes clearly to the former rather than to the latter. Weber, however, did not necessarily mean to defend capitalism on such grounds. Contrary to some current neo-Marxist interpretations of his thought Weber had no intention whatever of singing the praises of capitalism, let alone capitalism in its most 'formally rationalized' versions. The ideal-typical picture which Weber draws in *Economy and Society* of the pure type of a 'market economy' with maximum efficiency is not very attractive, and by no means identical with the form of capitalism which Weber was personally in favour of. In order to attain maximum formal rationality in an economic system the following essential conditions must be met:

(1) There ought to exist essentially unrestricted struggle between autonomous economic groups in the market. This amounts, in Weber's own words, to an economic version of the Darwinist principle of 'the struggle of man against man'. This is to say that only competition ought to decide on economic success or economic failure.

(2) It is necessary to have a money economy in which prices as well as capital costs, and consequently wages as well, are also accounted for rationally under the conditions of unrestricted competition in the market.

(3) There ought to be 'unrestricted market freedom', that is 'the absence of monopolies, which may be dictated by non-economic powers and hence of an irrational kind, or of a voluntary, and hence in economic terms rational (that is, market-oriented) quality'.[34]

(4) There ought to exist 'formally free labour', that is the workers are entitled to sell their working capacity freely (in a formally legal sense) in the market, and the entrepreneurs, on their part, are entitled to dispose of the labour of the workers whenever they think necessary.

(5) A further necessary prerequisite is the 'expropriation of the workers from the means of production. They must be dependent on the chance to seek earnings through labour only. This is to say, of course, that the appropriation of the means of production by the owners is to be protected by force.'[35]

(6) There should exist, last but not least, 'individual ownership'.

These are clearly conditions, which were not completely fulfilled in any of the capitalist societies of his time, if, indeed, they ever were. One may well wonder whether this had been the case even during the period of the so-called 'early capitalism', which in many ways obviously served as the pattern for the drawing up of such an ideal-type of the capitalist economy. To Weber this ideal-typical scheme was merely a marginal construct, whereas in empirical reality there will be found a great variety of market economies, most of them much less rationalized systems. He was fully aware, for instance, that the real face of capitalism in his own lifetime was to no small degree determined by all sorts of monopolies – something which, in principle, prevents capitalism from attaining a maximum of formal rationality. It would furthermore be completely wrong to suppose that Weber was particularly enthusiastic about the pure type of market economy which he had taken pains to outline without even the slightest attempt to hide any of its more unpleasant and inhuman features. Max Weber has recently been attacked by Herbert Marcuse for having identified the 'formal rationality' of capitalism with what may be called its 'substantive rationality' or, in Hegelian terms, its reason.[36] This is only partly justified, for Weber himself pointed out on various occasions, that 'formal rationality' and 'substantive rationality' are by no means identical, and, as a rule, not compatible with one another. 'Substantive rationality' meant, in Weber's terms, rationality not in a formal or instrumental sense. It refers to social systems or social institutions or even to forms of social conduct that are rationally oriented towards the realization of certain fundamental ideals as, for example, the principle of social justice. On one occasion Weber declared explicitly: 'The fact that the maximum of formal rationality in capital accounting is possible only provided that the workers are subjected to domination by the entrepreneurs is a further specific case of the substantive (*materiale*) irrationality of the (capitalist) economic system.'[37] That is to say that an economic system, which, in economic terms, is rationally organized throughout, can well be, and is indeed, extremely irrational, when analysed from the angle of particular value-positions. It must be admitted, however, that Weber never made this point sufficiently clear, and indeed allowed the impression to gain ground that not only 'formal rationality', but rationality as such can exist only in 'market economies' of the capitalist type. Hence it would follow, that rationality, and, indeed 'reason' were on the side of capitalism rather than that of other economic systems. Weber was, in fact, firmly convinced that all socialist economies – and the more radically they disposed of the regulative mechanism of the market, the more was this the case – had to face serious problems which resulted from the fundamental contradictions between 'formal' and 'substantive' rationality. Although he did not state this explicitly, this was in his eyes a key argument against the feasibility of socialist systems.

Weber contended that socialist economies would find it extremely difficult, if not impossible, to supplant the traditional economic incentives to do efficient work associated with the chances of personal gain by some sort of value-oriented incentives. As is now known, the present socialist systems certainly have problems of this nature, although they are still money economies. Weber warned, furthermore, that there was not the slightest reason to believe that, in nationalized economies, the workers would stop thinking in terms of their own individual economic advantage, all the more so as the actual economic position of the working classes in socialist systems would not be that much different from those under capitalism.[38]

It remains to be seen whether Weber's contention is correct that only economic systems which are market-oriented can attain a maximum of 'formal rationality' even in his sense; or whether the price which must be paid for this in the form of material irrationalities – like the subjection of the workers to the yoke of private employers, or the almost unavoidable growth of the economy in directions that are not desirable, for instance, for ecological reasons – is not too high. Yet it would be completely false to imply that Weber's option in favour of capitalism rather than socialism was due primarily to the fact that he was enthusiastic about the principle of the maximization of 'formal rationality' which only this economic system was capable of, as Herbert Marcuse among others would have it. Although at times Max Weber displayed a kind of aesthetic admiration for the rationalizing power of capitalism, he was increasingly worried about the dehumanizing consequences of purely formal rationalization. Indeed, he was scared of the craving of capitalism for 'formal rationality', which formed the basis of its 'unholy alliance' with bureaucratization – an alliance concluded regardless of the fact that in the long run capitalism, rather than bureaucracy, was bound to be the loser. Weber was not a champion of capitalism simply because he was an enthusiastic admirer of the capitalist system. In fact rather the opposite is true. With open eyes Weber analysed the working of the capitalist system as well as its social consequences, both in the short and the long term, and he was not inclined to make it appear better than it actually was. He perceived clearly that capitalism creates social trends which are detrimental to a humane social order. But he could not discover any easy way out of this. On the contrary, under given conditions capitalism still appeared to be relatively the best of all possible economic systems. The capitalist system was preferable to other economic systems especially, because it guaranteed a maximum degree of social dynamism and mobility. This was true in particular for those types of capitalist economies where the free entrepreneur, and possibly the highly qualified manager, can freely display their creative abilities, in contrast to those economies in which a dominant influence is given to the *rentiers* who dislike all social change for obvious reasons. For much the same reason he preferred a system in which the incomes of the employees, and other groups of dependent labour, were determined on the basis of free contracts rather than according to a rigid system of fixed wages and salaries.[39] On the other hand, he strongly demanded that the workers should enjoy a fair bargaining position, if necessary guaranteed by means of adequate social legislation.

Both his liberal convictions and far-reaching considerations about the future of Western societies made Max Weber infinitely prefer dynamic capitalism, despite its shortcomings, to all kinds of socialist economies. In two respects his case against socialism was a good one: first, in so far as he argued that it was not the ownership of property as such, but rather the control of the entrepreneurial positions which matters; secondly, when he pointed out that the real cause of the 'alienation', not only of the working classes, but of the great majority of the population in modern societies, lay in the emerging bureaucratic structures and not so much in the particular modes of the distribution of wealth. At least in this latter respect history has largely been on his side. The abolition of the private appropriation of the means of production may possibly pave the way for a proper solution to the pressing problems of modern society, but it is just as likely to make things worse. Weber did not suggest ways and means and ways to achieve a proper system for the control of complex industrial societies in the interests of preserving human values, but at least he pointed to some of the decisive issues. It therefore seems fully justified to call him a bourgeois thinker par excellence who matched the greatness of his Marxist antipode.[40]

Notes

1. Cf. Albert Salomon, 'Max Weber', in: *Die Gesellschaft*, Vol. III, 1, 1926, p. 131.
2. Cf. Karl Löwith, 'Max Weber and Karl Marx', in: *Gesammelte Abhandlungen zur Kritik der geschichtlichen Existenz*, Stuttgart, 1960, p. 3f; W. A. Runciman, *Social Science and Political Theory*, Cambridge, 1965, pp. 52f.

3. For Honigsheim see his essay: 'Max Weber in Heidelberg. Erinnerungen an Max Weber', in: *Max Weber zum Gedächtnis. Kölner Zeitschrift für Soziologie und Sozialpsychologie*, Sonderheft 7, 1963, pp. 161ff., as well as his *On Max Weber. Collected Essays*, New York, 1968.

4. 'Der Sozialismus', *Gesammelte Aufsätze zur Soziologie und Sozialpolitik*, Tübingen, 1924 (henceforth referred to as *SSP*), pp. 492ff. For a detailed analysis of the political context of this public speech see W. J. Mommsen, *Max Weber*, p. 276f.

5. Cf., for instance, Günther Roth, 'Das historische Verhältnis der Weberschen Soziologie zum Marxismus', *Kölner Zeitschrift für Soziologie*, Vol. XX, 3, 1968, p. 432; ibid., 'The Historical Relationship to Marxism', in: Reinhard Bendix and Guenther Roth, *Scholarship and Partisanship: Essays on Max Weber*, University of California Press, Berkeley, 1971, pp. 227ff. Anthony Giddens, *Capitalism and Modern Social Theory. An Analysis of the Writings of Marx, Durkheim and Max Weber*, Cambridge, 1971, pp. 190ff. gives a short outline of Weber's attitude towards Marx, but does not discuss the essential problem of capitalism versus bureaucratic socialism.

6. See above, pp. 2ff.

7. *Shils*, p. 68.

8. Cf. Jürgen Kocka, 'Karl Marx und Max Weber. Ein methodologischer Vergleich', *Zeitschrift für die gesammte Staatswissenschaft*, Vol. 122, 1966, pp. 341f. Richard Ashcraft, 'Marx and Weber on Liberalism as Bourgeois Ideology', *Comparative Studies in Society and History*, Vol. 14, No. 2, 1972, shows strikingly the similarities between Weber's and Marx's approach, regardless of the former's reservations as to Marx's dogmatic method.

9. This point has to be made against the argument of Kocka, op. cit., p. 344, which tends to take the earlier methodological writings as the whole story.

10. Cf. W. J. Mommsen, *Max Weber*, p. 121f.

11. *SSP*, p. 456. See also *WL*, p. 315.

12. *WL*, pp. 299ff.

13. Cf. *Lebensbild*, p. 652.

14. Cf. *RS*, Vol. 1, p. 252: 'Interessen (materielle und ideelle), nicht: Ideen, beherrschen unmittelbar das Handeln der Menschen.'

15. See note 2, above.

16. Cf. Löwith, op. cit., pp. 35ff.

17. *WuG*, Vol. 1, p. 79 (trans. by the author). Cf. *EaS*, Vol. 1, p. 139.

18. *PS*, p. 337f.

19. Ibid.

20. *PS*, p. 333. Cf. the differently worded trans. by Roth in *EaS*, Vol. 3, p. 1403.

21. *SSP*, p. 508.

22. See, for instance letter to Midiels, 4th Aug. 1908, quoted in Mommsen, *Max Weber*, p. II8.

23. *WuG*, Vol. 2, p. 531 (*EaS*, Vol. 2, p. 927.)

24. *WuG*, Vol. 1, p. 177f.

25. One is tempted to apply this ideal-typical concept to the present-day communist systems of orthodox Marxist-Leninist allegiance.

26. *WuG*, Vol. 1, p. 178 (*EaS*, Vol. 1, p. 304.)

27. *WuG*, Vol. 1, p. 179 (*EaS*, Vol. 1, p. 305.) This passage should be interpreted in connexion with *SSP*, p. 509f., where Weber takes a slightly different position regarding the process of disintegration of the working class.

28. *WuG*, Vol. 1, p. 179f. (*EaS*, Vol. 1, p. 305f.).

29. *WuG*, Vol. 2, p. 533. The trans. given by Roth in *EaS*, Vol. 2, p. 930 is somewhat misleading.

30. *WuG*, p. 59f. (*EaS*, Vol. 1, pp. 109ff.)

31. *WuG*, Vol. 1, p. 59 (author's trans.). Cf. trans. by Roth, *EaS*, Vol. 1, p. 109, which does not fully bring out the meaning of the passage.

32. *WuG*, Vol. 1, p. 61 (*EaS*, Vol. 1, p. 112). Weber here refers directly to Marx's *Misère de la Philosophie*.

33. Ibid., p. 60 (*EaS*, Vol. 1, p. 111).

34. *WuG*, Vol. 1, p. 58. Cf. *EaS*, Vol. 1, p. 108 (Roth's trans. modified by the author).
35. *WuG*, Vol. 1, p. 87. The trans. by Roth in *EaS*, Vol. 1, p. 115, gives the meaning of this passage only vaguely.
36. Herbert Marcuse launched in 1964 on the *Soziologentag* at Heidelberg a most impressive attack on Weber. He argued that Max Weber identifies the 'formal rationality' of the capitalist system with 'rationality' as such, and that Weber for this very reason ended up with a solution which, although it was presented as a rational one, or more precisely, as the only rational one, was indeed irrational to the highest degree. See Herbert Marcuse, 'Industrialisation and Capitalism', *New Left Review*, Vol. 30, 1965, pp. 2ff; also in Stammer, op. cit., pp. 133ff. See also the controversy about Marcuse's paper, ibid., pp. 152ff. Marcuse's arguments are taken up, however, in a somewhat dogmatic manner, by Wolfgang Lefèvre, *Zum historischen Charakter und zur historischen Funktion der Methode bürgerlicher Soziologie*, Frankfurt, 1971, especially pp. 33f, and 56f. Lefèvre argues that Weber's identification of capitalism with 'formal rationality' was nothing other than a bourgeois strategy designed to serve as an apology for the capitalist system. He claims that Weber did not base his formalist judgements about society on any sort of rationality 'in den Inhalten der Wirklichkeit' (ibid., p. 56). He, in turn, takes refuge in a kind of Marxist *naïveté* which assumes that once all forms of domination have been abolished a substantially rational social system will of necessity emerge. Hence he absolves himself from the duty of demonstrating why his line of reasoning is, as he claims, the only one possible, and why it alone concurs with social reality. Much more to the point is Jürgen Habermas' reply to Marcuse, *Technik und Wissenschaft als Ideologie*, Frankfurt, 1970, pp. 48ff. Elaborating upon the arguments of Marcuse, Habermas analyses the concept of *technische Rationalität*, which is derived from Weber's 'formal rationality' of social institutions, and points out that it may indeed serve as a means of justifying domination in 'late-capitalist societies'. Yet, on the other hand, he shows that Marcuse's protest against the principle of 'formal rationality' is utopian, in so far as it is impossible to dispose of 'technical rationality' under the conditions of modern industrial production. As is shown above, Marcuse's criticism of the 'formal rationality' of capitalism is much closer to Weber's own argumentation than he himself was aware of. It is worth noting that none of the scholars who spoke up passionately in defence of Max Weber in the Heidelberg conference realized this.
37. *WuG*, Vol. 1, p. 78 (author's trans.; cf. *EaS*, Vol. 1, p. 138).
38. *WuG*, Vol. 1, p. 88f. (*EaS*, Vol. 1, p. 116f.); *WuG*, Vol. 1, p. 119f. (*EaS*, p. 202f.)
39. *WuG*, Vol. 1, p. 121 (author's trans.; cf. *EaS*, Vol. 1, p. 205): 'Of all types of income it is particularly those from entrepreneurial profits or from labour incomes derived either from contracts agreed upon either according to piece rates or from contracts made by free agreement, which have an eminently dynamic – that is to say revolutionary – effect on the economic system.'
40. I cannot quite agree with Ashcraft, op. cit., p. 168, that Weber failed to develop a theory of bourgeois society, although he is correct in saying that Weber was too much tied to the liberal tradition to reflect the liberal system in all its respects. All the essential elements of a theory of liberal bourgeois capitalism are, in my opinion, there:
    1. that an economy organized on the lines of private ownership of the means of production, as well as 'formally free labour' is capable of attaining a maximum of success with regard to the production of goods.
    2. that the struggle of men against men in the market results not only in a maximum of 'formal rationality' of the system, but also of productivity, whereas other forms of economic organization tend to be more or less static.
    3. that amongst all possible economic systems the sort of capitalist economy which gives priority to entrepreneurial profits as well as to income from formally free contracts, and which provides for a maximum of competition on the market, develops a maximum of economic, and hence also social and political, dynamism; that is to say, it provides the most favourable conditions for an 'open society'.

CHAPTER 4

The Theory of the 'Three Pure Types of Legitimate Domination' and the Concept of Plebiscitarian Democracy

Max Weber's theory of the 'three pure types of legitimate domination'[1] is probably the most famous part of his political sociology.[2] Indeed, it forms the central core of his reasoning about the various types of domination throughout world history. It should be understood that the 'three pure types of legitimate domination' do not apply only to the modern state; in principle they deal with all forms of power relationships of whatever kind. It was an attempt to construct an 'ideal-typical' systematization which would allow one to determine, as well as analyse, any given concrete case of domination from the point of view of certain fundamental issues related to those problems which Weber considered to be of universal significance. These included particularly the question of leadership in a bureaucratic world, or the relevance of systems of bureaucratic rule for an individualistic liberalism.

The theory of the 'three pure types of legitimate domination', or more precisely, the ideal-typical systematization of types of legitimate rule, is perhaps the most mature and elaborate part of Max Weber's universal interpretative sociology. It was developed on the basis of a comparative analysis of various forms of domination throughout all known past history. It is, in fact, as much theoretical history as historical sociology, if only in so far as it claims to serve as a yardstick for the evaluation of any sort of domination, whether in the remote past or in present day societies.

At first sight the 'three pure types of legitimate domination' have little to do with the course of world history. They appear to be altogether static. 'Legal domination' by means of bureaucratic administrative techniques; 'traditional domination' by means of an administrative staff consisting of men who are personally dependent on the ruler; and 'charismatic domination', that is the rule of a charismatic leader by means of a retinue unreservedly devoted to him as a person endowed with unusual qualities; these three different types do not appear to be linked with one another in any way whatsoever. Weber took pains to make clear that these types of rule do not necessarily follow one another. The theory of the 'three pure types of legitimate domination' was not intended to be a scheme which stood for a sort of linear perspective of world history leading from charismatic forms of government at the beginning, to bureaucratic forms of government at the very end. Neither had it anything to do with the various versions of a circular theory of world history. Weber deliberately put the type of 'bureaucratic domination' first, if only to forestall any such misunderstandings – although in the earlier versions there are some allusions to the idea that charismatic forms of domination are predominant in earlier periods of history, whereas bureaucratic forms are comparatively recent products of universal history. In the latest version, however, Weber systematically cut out all allusions to particular historical events, or pushed them into the role of a mere commentary; the factor of historical time was deliberately eliminated.[3] Weber also went to some lengths to make it clear that none of these 'pure types' was ever actually to be found in historical or social reality. At most one could discover close approximations to them. This follows, of course, from the logical nature of the 'ideal type' which, in Weber's understanding, is a purely mental construct designed to bring to light precisely those aspects of reality which are most significant. All forms of domination encountered in empirical reality are mixtures of these three pure types, although in greatly varying combinations. Weber maintained that only by approaching empirical reality with such clear-cut ideal-typical constructs can the social scientist find a path through the confusing maze of often conflicting empirical data.

All this being so it is worth noting that the theory of 'the three pure types of legitimate domination' nonetheless bears the imprint of its intellectual origins, which may be traced back as far as Aristotle's theory of three forms of government circulating from monarchy to oligarchy and democracy and again to monarchy. Weber was probably stimulated to attempt the construction of such a general scheme of types of domination by August Wilhelm Roscher's *Politik. Geschichtliche Naturlehre der Monarchie, Aristokratie und Demokratie* which had been published in 1892 and which stood within the tradition of the circular theories handed down through the ages from Aristotle via Polybius and Machiavelli to Vico and Hegel, and which had been taken up again by German neo-romanticism. It was against this background that Weber took pains to eliminate everything from his own systematization which would appear to be of a teleological nature. The 'three types of legitimate domination' were intended to be the opposite of a construction of world history in the traditional sense; rather, they were meant to be purely structural models of possible types of dominations.

Yet even if this is accepted, it can be hardly overlooked that the theory of the 'three pure types of legitimate domination' has at least two things in common with the traditional theories just mentioned:

First, in so far as it claims to be a comprehensive theory, that is, that it is applicable to all known types of domination throughout history.

Secondly, in so far as it tends to associate each type of domination not only with a corresponding type of political culture (which would imply that its validity is by no means limited to politics and statesmanship alone) but also with a particular economic system, and finally with a particular kind of civilization. This becomes obvious if we draw up a systematic scheme of the three 'pure types' and the respective types of legal order as well as the prevailing forms of social conduct associated with them. This may be gathered from the graph on pages 76–7.[4]

	The Three Types of Legal Domination	
	According to instrumentally-rationally enacted rules	According to value-rational rules (for instance 'Natural Law')
Head of the System (type of 'master')	Official (civil servant)	Elected official(s) or collegiate body
Source of the authority of the head of the system (or 'master')	Official (civil servant)	Elected official(s) or collegiate body
Form of legitimacy of the System	Belief in the formal correctness of the enacted system of rules because it has been agreed upon by the interested parties because it was enacted or imposed by an authority considered to be legitimated to do so (it is all important that the rules are enacted in a formally correct manner)	Value-rational belief in the validity of the basic principles of the system of rules. The laws are considered merely explications of the fundamental principles
Type of administrative staff	Bureaucracy	Bureaucracy, or elected civil servants

Type of legal system	Instrumentally-rational formal law, enacted according to positivistic principles	Value-rational law, founded and derived from fundamental principles, yet otherwise strictly formal
Predominant type of social conduct	Instrumentally-rational social conduct	Value-rational social conduct

Legitimate Domination

	Traditional Domination	*Charismatic Domination*
Patriarchal rule	Estate-type rule	
Monarch or religious dignitary	Monarch or religious dignitary	Prophet, warlord, demagogue, leader
Tradition, or heredity, often supported by religious rituals	Tradition, or heredity, often supported by religious rituals	Emotional devotion of the 'retinue' to the charismatic leader (which is considered a duty that can be enforced by the leader)
	Belief in the prescriptive order of things	Affectual or emotional belief in the extraordinary qualities of the charismatic leader, and in the values revealed by him
Personnel personally dependent of the head of the system ('Servants of the master')	Offices are appropriated either by tradition or by the representatives of an estate	Retinue of the leader all officials are personally devoted to the charismatic leader
Strictly traditional, yet material in its judication	Strictly traditional law, judicated in a formalist procedure	The ruler imposes or modifies the law at his discretion
Traditional social conduct	Traditional social conduct	Affectual, in particular cases: value-rational social conduct

It has to be admitted, however, that Weber tended, in the later versions of his work, to formulate the theory of 'the three pure types of legitimate domination' more and more in purely instrumental terms in order to make it applicable to political phenomena of smaller dimensions. A systematic analysis of the three 'pure types' reveals that, contrary to our initial impression, a distinctive 'ideal-typical' interdependence exists between them which in some ways makes up for a major deficiency of this systemization, namely, the apparently static nature of the 'pure types of legitimate domination'. First, the type of 'charismatic domination' enjoys an importance out of all proportion to its actual part in history. Yet it is by no means a mere coincidence that a dominant role is assigned to the type of charismatic domination; this is due to the very nature of charisma. Charisma is, to Weber, the source of all creative individual leadership, and for that very reason no other type of political domination, be it predominantly traditional or of purely bureaucratic cast – can ever work without at least an element of charisma. As Reinhard Bendix has aptly put it, the concept of 'charisma' is the archetype of Weber's political sociology.[5] What did Weber actually mean by introducing this nowadays rather controversial concept into his political sociology? 'Charisma' is, in the first place, the quality which identifies a particular person as a leader in the eyes of those around him. Weber had derived this concept from the usage of the early Christian communities, where charisma was considered a divine gift, by which God himself had designated certain persons as leaders. However, Weber substituted for the religious meaning of the concept a phenomeno-logical one, which referred only to the capability of a charismatic leader to rally to himself a retinue of devoted followers. Weber defined charisma in a formalist, supposedly value-free way: charisma is the quality of a person which creates a willingness in his followers to subject themselves uncondi-tionally to his leadership. They accept his leadership because they believe in his personal qualifications as a leader per se, whatever his particular goals may be. Weber observed that the attachment of the followers to the leader was of a personal and hence highly emotional kind. Indeed, the emotional and personal character of the relationship between the leader and his retinue was, in his opinion, the main reason for the peculiar insta-bility of 'charismatic rule'. A charismatic leader has to prove his qualifica-tion for leadership anew every day, and a good deal of success is therefore essential for maintaining his position. It is somewhat irritating to note that, in the last resort, success 'is the main, although possibly not the only, criterion by which a leader may be judged charismatic. A leader who fails, who does not live up to the expectations which he himself has created in the minds of his retinue, is likely to lose his charismatic appeal all of a sud-den. His retinue disbands, his followers desert him.

Although Weber treated charismatic leadership in the context of his political sociology as just one particular type among others, he nonethe-less showed a strong tendency to identify it with genuine leadership of any kind. This is in line with Weber's own personal convictions regarding the role of the individual in history. Weber's charismatic personalities have much in common with Nietzsche's great individuals who set new values for themselves and for their followers, in a heroic attempt to elevate man-kind to a higher level.[6]

The notion that all genuine leadership is, in some way or another, of a charismatic nature, does indeed lead to the conclusion that some element of 'charisma', whether in a routinized or in a disguised form, is required in every system of domination, regardless of its particular nature. Weber pointed out time and again that the strength and, incidentally, the stability of bureaucratic governments of the legal type depends on whether the system allows dynamic personalities with charismatic, that is to say: 'leadership' qualities to obtain the top positions. For they alone, and not the officials, are capable of setting goals and objectives which are then to be 'sold' to the people at large by 'party machines', and afterwards implemented with the help of administrative bureaucracies. Weber emphasised repeatedly the fundamental difference between the official and the political leader: the former is supposed only to administer in accordance with the enacted system of legal norms, whereas the latter ought to give a lead to the administration, as well as to mobilize adequate support from the people at large. Most of the evils of Wilhelmian Germany, for instance, were, according to Weber, due to the fact that this essential truth had been disregarded constantly. Much the same was also the case with regard to the economic system, although Weber did not explicitly say so in this context. A dynamic economy could not get along without the economic leadership qualities of private entrepreneurs.

There is, however, one fundamental difficulty which must be faced. Weber never distinguished clearly between charismatic leadership and charismatic 'domination', largely because he had a tendency to define domination (*Herrschaft*) in more or less personalistic terms, as will be shown later. Strictly speaking a type of charismatic domination is an impossibility, for pure charisma loathes any form of institutionalization; it is a purely ephemeral phenomenon. Yet it is important to see that the concept of 'charisma' nevertheless plays a decisive role in Weber's theory of legitimate types of domination. It is, in fact, the main element providing a link between the three types of domination. In Weber's *Interpretive Sociology* the following ideal-typical patterns of dynamic change are encountered by which one particular pure type of legitimate rule may be transformed into, or at least blended, with another:

First, revolutionary break-throughs brought about by the determined action of charismatic personalities and their retinues in the face of a traditionalist environment. Such a dynamic break-through, as a rule, results in the establishment of a kind of charismatic rule.

Secondly, the 'routinization' of revolutionary 'charisma' which, in due course, transmutes a charismatic system into a tradition-bound society, either of a patriarchal or of the more common type of patrimonial domination. This is the most significant, and perhaps the most common form of historical change. Thirdly, another secular force of social change is found, namely rationalization, or to be more precise formal rationalization, by which tradition-bound or value-oriented forms of political and social organization are gradually replaced by purely instrumentally-rational institutions. In doing so rationalization displays two imminent tendencies of great force: The tendency to maximize formal efficiency, and the tendency to stabilize the system, so as to make further far-reaching political and social change extremely difficult.

Weber points out that the process of rationalization has often been initiated by revolutionary action, either of the value-rational or of the charismatic type – the former can be illustrated by the Puritan sects who invented the ideology of the 'Rights of Man', and also created modern capitalism. The most conspicuous example of revolutionary action of the charismatic type which leads to rationalization is shown, according to Weber, by the Jewish prophets. By demanding the most extraordinary things from the Jewish people they prompted their followers to subject their own lives to an iron law of rational social conduct. Weber makes the further allowance that the process of 'rationalization' may, in particular cases, retain its original association with particular value-attitudes. As a rule, however, it almost always takes a different direction, inasmuch as it paves the way for the universal advance of purely instrumentally-oriented social institutions, to the detriment of all value-oriented forms of social conduct.

It is the most significant feature of all 'instrumentally-rational' social systems that they operate exclusively according to the principle of pure formal legality, rather than according to such legal principles as are derived from, and dependent on, a particular set of ultimate values. Unfortunately Weber was never very outspoken on this point, largely because he acted upon the assumption that all value-oriented versions of legality – the most conspicuous case being 'Natural Law' – were in any case dwindling away. At least in modern industrial society they appeared to have lost all of their concrete meaning. The 'disenchantment of the world' closely associated with the progress of modern science as well as the irresistible advance of bureaucratization left less and less room for value-oriented forms of domination.

It is worth noting, furthermore, that Weber strongly emphasized the purely formal quality of legality, as the dominant feature of the type of legal domination. It is belief in the formally correct enactment of any laws which establishes their legitimacy whereas the substantive values which they may represent play merely a marginal role. Weber constructed the 'pure type of legal domination' as the dialectical counterpart of 'charismatic domination' and therefore in the later sections of his work deliberately cut out all references to the possible case that the legitimacy of the system is derived from certain fundamental value-oriented attitudes of the 'governed', as is the case with the traditional doctrine of democracy.

Weber gloomily depicted the kind of society which would come closest to a full implementation of all the elements listed under the type of pure legal rule. It would be administered by an almighty bureaucracy in accordance with a closely knit network of laws and regulations of a purely formalistic nature, which would leave little or no space for individually oriented creative action. In such a system all moral values would be of little avail, for the organizational structure would only take into account technical considerations, without any regard to the value attitudes of the particular groups or individuals concerned. The trend toward bureaucratization was, in Weber's opinion, almost irresistible. For bureaucratic machines tend to submit everything to strict rational rules if only in order continuously to extend their own sphere of control. It does not need much imagination to realize, that eventually all individual initiative would be suffocated by the iron force of a network of purely instrumentally-legal stipulations. The political system would become oppressive, and the economy would gradually lose all its dynamism and would eventually become a stationary system.

Yet however much he was haunted by these prospects, and although he was aware of the fact that bureaucracies belong among those things in the world which are almost indestructible, Max Weber did not rule out the possibility of partial charismatic break-throughs even in highly bureaucratized societies. This does not mean that he looked for the emergence of new charismatic forms of domination as such. Yet there was always the chance that, in particular sectors of bureaucratic societies, qualified personalities would emerge with the charismatic gift to set new goals for the social institutions and to secure a sufficient degree of support from the masses in order to be enabled to implement these goals by political means. By making use of the technological facilities available (for instance, the party machines) they would be able to give new impulses to social systems which were otherwise bound to become stationary. Consequently Weber strongly favoured such social and political structures as would allow the rise of charismatic leaders to influence and power, within a framework of legal rule and bureaucratic organization. Weber believed that the plebiscitarian rule of great democratic leaders would best meet these requirements. As will be shown below in somewhat more detail, it is primarily for this reason that he eventually became a passionate champion of what he himself called the 'plebiscitarian leader-democracy'.

Max Weber considered the 'plebiscitarian democracy' the only viable form in which democracy was possible under the conditions prevailing in industrial mass societies. What place did he assign to this type of rule in his theory of the 'three pure types of legitimate domination'? It turns out to be rather difficult to find a proper place for modern 'plebiscitarian democracy' in this elaborate schematization – a fact which has troubled quite a few scholars who have attempted to interpret Weber's political sociology in the light of our faith in a system of 'constitutional democracy', which guarantees freedom to all individuals, Before we embark upon this difficult problem the question must be raised why Weber throughout his work always spoke of 'legitimate domination' without ever giving consideration to possible types of 'illegitimate domination'. What is the position with regard to classical tyranny, or the various authoritarian systems of his own day, or even the modern totalitarian systems of the Fascist or Communist varieties? The concept of 'illegitimate rule' turns up in Weber's sociology only once and there it refers to the medieval city state that has emancipated itself from the political control of a former overlord, who – speaking in terms of the medieval tradition – was the only source which could confer legitimacy on another political authority.[7]

This has clearly nothing to do with the theory of the 'three pure types of legitimate domination'. In fact, one cannot escape the conclusion that in the context of Weber's sociological theory of 'legitimate rule' there was no room for illegitimate forms of domination. This kind of conceptualization apparently does not allow a distinction between what would nowadays be called government by consent on the one hand and tyrannical dictatorships which force people into submission by means of manipulation or oppression on the other. The reason why Weber talks constantly of 'legitimate' domination can only be explained, to some degree, on the grounds that he approached the phenomenon of 'domination' in a purely functionalist manner. 'Power' (Macht) and 'domination' (Herrschaft) are defined in an extremely formalistic way and at the same time in probabilistic terms:

'"Power" (*Macht*) is the probability (*Chance*) that one actor within a social relationship will be in a position to carry out his own will despite resistance, whatever the basis of this probability may be.' '"Domination" (*Herrschaft*) is the probability that a command with a given specific content will be obeyed by a given group of persons.'[8] Or, as Weber puts it in another context, '"domination" as a sociological concept . . . can only mean that there is a chance that the governed will submit to any command' (*für einen Befehl Fügsamheit zu finden*).[9] From these definitions we may gather the specific meaning of 'legitimacy' with regard to the various types of 'domination'. It refers to the motivations which induce the subjects (or 'governed') to obey the commands given to them by the ruler, regardless of whether these commands are addressed to them personally or, as is more often the case, are couched in the abstract language of regulations, laws or orders in council. The probability that any command will be obeyed by a given group of persons depends, according to Weber, largely on one thing, namely whether they believe in the legitimacy of the system or not. Yet if we try to push the issue further in order to find substantive reasons why and under which conditions a system may be legitimate, we hit a vacuum. We are told that there are three different types of such beliefs, but that is about all. Legitimacy, in Weber's terms, amounts to little more than an equivalent of the stability of the respective political system. In other words there cannot be other than 'legitimate' systems of 'domination'. If the 'governed' do not believe in the legitimacy of a political system it is bound to be unstable, and will eventually collapse. Conversely, a stable system of domination must *ipso facto* be supported by those who are governed by it.[10] Unfortunately Weber did not analyse this problem any further, and it may be said, that his deliberately functionalist approach did not allow him to do so. From this it follows that the very attempt to present a comprehensive ideal-typical scheme of types of legitimate domination was of necessity associated with some substantive deficiencies.

Weber was, of course, fully justified in not embarking upon a value-oriented discussion of the problems of legitimacy. Yet the problem remains with us that stability – and this is just another word for success – is, in the last resort, the decisive criterion of whether a political system may be considered legitimate or not. There is simply no room for even ephemeral forms of illegitimate domination. A political system which is not legitimate in either of the three forms, is, on the basis of Weber's conceptualization, bound to collapse at once, and, conversely, any stable government, whatever it may be like, must be legitimate in some way or another.

It could be argued that the 'three pure types of legitimate domination' are incompatible with one another and that therefore a political system which, say, belongs to the type of patriarchal domination is illegitimate in the light of charismatic or bureaucratic principles. Yet Weber did not think so.[11] He pointed out again and again that the legitimacy of all empirically known systems of domination rests on mixed foundations, that is, on a combination of all three sources of legitimacy, although, as a rule, one of them plays the dominant role. Neither can systems of 'charismatic rule' attain even a minimum of stability without elements of 'traditional' and even 'bureaucratic legitimacy', nor can bureaucratic systems survive for long without the additional support of substantial elements of both 'traditional' and 'charismatic legitimacy'.

Hence it follows that there is no easy escape from the problems which arise from this deliberately functionalist conceptualization. Attempts to modify it somewhat – for instance, by adding a fourth type of 'legitimate rule' which applied specifically to all democratic systems of domination – are bound to come to nothing.[12] The vital question of how we are to distinguish between political systems which we consider legitimate in so far as they rest on the consent of the people, and others which are more or less oppressive will not find any answer on these grounds. First because Weber deliberately abstained from any value-oriented discussion of legitimacy, and secondly because he seems to have assumed, as a matter of course, that every stable system appears to enjoy the consent of the 'governed', although it might have a very different quality in each case.

From the sociological point of view this is a thoroughly justified approach, although it fails to produce any criteria which would enable us to distinguish between free and oppressive systems of domination. It may be further argued that Weber was not so much concerned with this problem because his own conception of 'democratic rule' was almost as functionalist as his sociological theory of domination. Weber was an advocate of democracy on the grounds that, under the social and political conditions of a modern bureaucratic society, it offered a maximum of dynamism and leadership. The classical democratic doctrine, however, meant little to him. He did not at all believe in the theory of the sovereignty of the people. In 1908 he wrote to Robert Michels who at the time was working hard to find an answer to the question of how to reconcile the ethical postulate of the sovereignty of the people with a reality that gave birth to ever new oligarchies: 'How much resignation will you still have to put up with? Such concepts as "will of the people", genuine will of the people, have long since ceased to exist for me; they are fictitious. All ideas aiming at abolishing the dominance of men over men are "Utopian".'[13] For Weber, parliamentary democracy was anything but the realization of the principle of self-determination of the people. This was, in his opinion, mere ideological trash. Its main purpose consisted in bringing politicians with genuinely charismatic qualifications – that is to say qualified political leaders rather than narrow-minded bureaucrats – into power.

In this context the parliamentary bodies had to play a twofold role. First, they were, as Weber put it, an ideal training ground for genuine political leaders. Secondly, the parliamentary bodies had to keep the administrative bureaucracies in check, if need be by setting up special committees of inquiry. Otherwise, Weber assigned to the parliamentary bodies a rather passive role. The parliament as such was not supposed to determine the actual course in politics, not even in a very general sense. It is, according to Weber, the great political leaders who create for themselves a majority in parliament as well as amongst the people at large, and do so not so much on the basis of a positive programme, but by displaying their charismatic power of persuasion and positive demagogy.

Weber did not hesitate to describe all leadership in a modern 'plebiscitarian democracy' in charismatic terms. The mass of the delegates, as well as the people at large, are expected to follow the political leader; not so much because he stands for a particular issue, but because they believe in his personal leadership qualities. Weber stated quite bluntly that the people at large are, in fact, incapable of judging the political issues at stake on their real merits. They follow those political leaders who put the issue in the most convincing manner. Hence the democratic process is essentially a competitive struggle of various political leaders for the support of the people in which their respective 'positive demagogic' capacities are of crucial importance. This is clearly the liberal model of competition which is transplanted by Weber from economics to the field of parliamentary mass democracy. With it goes the assumption that the eventual victor in this competition is not only likely to be the most qualified leader, in the formal sense, but also that his political programme is the best as well. It is a necessary consequence of this theory of democratic rule that the representative bodies are assigned a strictly secondary role in the process of decision-making. By and large they have only the function merely of a counterweight to the uninhibited initiative of the political leaders. The necessity of keeping a parliamentary majority together amounts to a continuous testing of their charismatic leadership qualities. Moreover, they are constantly reminded of their particular responsibilities through the parliamentary struggle. Apart from that, the parliamentary machinery offers an ideal solution of the problem of the succession of leaders. As soon as a political leader shows signs of a lack of leadership, that is, if his charismatic qualities are waning, it is up to the parliamentary bodies to see that he is replaced by a new, better qualified leader.

Weber admitted that modern 'plebiscitarian democracy', in which a dominant role is allotted to charismatic leaders who compete with one another for power by means of a positive demagogy, was largely emotional. He pointed out that in a plebiscitarian democracy 'the devotion to and the trust in the leader are, as a rule, 'inevitably of an emotional nature'.[14] He accepted this as an indisputable fact. He was convinced that in modern bureaucratic societies only the great demagogue could successfully establish real leadership. Only by appealing directly to the masses, instead of taking advice from the administrative bureaucracies, will the great politician be allowed to pursue a farsighted and daring policy.

Weber further strengthened his case by pointing out that such a 'charismatic leadership' was not simply a postulate; it had long since emerged as a consequence of fundamental changes in the nature of modern democracy. The extension of the franchise and the development of highly organized party machines had long since swept aside the old liberal conception of parliament as a virtual elite of the nation which decides on matters of national policy by rational deliberation, regardless of party affiliations. It is only in a formal sense that parliament still retains its place as the only legitimate body where all political decisions were made. In fact, the party organizations had long ago taken over the actual control of parliamentary as well as all other political business. It is they rather than parliament which henceforth articulate the political issues – with an eye on the prospects of winning for and through them public support. Hence decisions arrived at by debate and rational deliberation were gradually superseded by plebiscitarian decisions. At the same time new types of political leaders emerged who were capable of appealing directly to the masses. Henceforth the people no longer chose between political issues and programmes but merely between the political leaders who have the task of convincing the masses of the righteousness of their cause, and in doing so they are expected to make use of their charismatic and demagogic capabilities.

The emergence of great plebiscitarian leaders or, as Weber puts it in *Politics as a Vocation*, of 'dictators of the battlefield of elections' was in his opinion the definitive step leading towards 'plebiscitarian democracy'[15] Only the 'plebiscitarian dictator' who rallies the masses behind him by means of his charismatic appeal, can establish leadership in a society where bureaucratic institutions are extending their operations to every section of human activity. This implies, however, that the members of parliament are reduced to mere 'political spoilsmen enrolled in his following'.[16] Referring to the political situation in Germany in 1919, Weber made the following diagnosis: 'There is, however, only the choice between leader-democracy with a "machine" [i.e. a highly bureaucratized party organization which is completely subservient to the political leader], and leaderless democracy, that is to say the rule of professional politicians without a calling, i.e. without the inner charismatic qualities that make a leader.'[17] 'Leader-democracy' means the charismatic rule of great political personalities within the framework of a democratic constitution. 'Leaderless democracy' means a form of democratic rule in which everything is handled merely as a matter of routine.[18]

At this point we may again take up the question of what place the concept of modern plebiscitarian democracy holds in Weber's ideal-typical theory of 'legitimate domination'. One would expect that modern constitutional democracy of whatever type would have to be subsumed under the heading of 'legal rule', if only because all its operations are performed in the form of legislative procedures and various forms of legislation. Max Weber, however, did not think so. His solution is highly characteristic of his own reasoning, and only understandable if one takes into account the key importance he attributed to the problems of political leadership in modern bureaucratic societies. In contrast to earlier tendencies in his writings, Weber considered modern plebiscitarian democracy to be essentially different from most traditional types of democracy. In one of the later sections of 'Economy and Society', written about 1919, he defines it as an anti-authoritarian version of 'charismatic domination': 'Plebiscitarian democracy, the most important type of leader-democracy, is, in its genuine sense, a sort of charismatic rule concealed behind a legitimacy which is formally derived from the will of the governed, and dependent upon it for its existence. In fact, the leader (demagogue) rules by virtue of the devotion [of his followers] and their confidence in him as a person.'[19] Weber went to some lengths to make it clear that this did not necessarily amount to an irrational interpretation of plebiscitarian democracy. He argued that 'the anti-authoritarian interpretation of charisma normally leads into the path of rationality'.[20] He apparently assumed that charismatic leadership is, in principle, fully compatible with an otherwise 'instrumentally-legal' political system. Nonetheless a classification of 'plebiscitarian democracy' under the type of charismatic legitimacy is somewhat surprising, even if full weight is given to Weber's argument that in a democratic system the power of a charismatic leader depends on the formal consent of the ruled. For one, it is arguable whether the issue of leadership is as decisive as Weber would have it. Secondly, it seems difficult to reconcile with the idea of democracy Weber's contention that the charismatic leader is, strictly speaking, responsible only to himself and that it is he who must convince the electorate with his 'positive' demagogy, rather than act according to their will.

Nevertheless, one is perhaps justified in following Max Weber in the interpretation of modern plebiscitarian democracy as an anti-authoritarian version of charismatic rule, in so far as some more recent trends in Western democratic systems would seem to corroborate his analysis. Among other political scientists Lowenstein has pointed this out. Yet, if this is so, the question of what 'charisma' is really supposed to be becomes all the more important.

Many scholars have been puzzled by the fact that Weber's ideal-typical theory of 'charisma' does not allow any distinction between the 'genuine charisma of responsible democratic leaders, as for instance, Gladstone or Roosevelt, and the pernicious charisma of personalities like Kurt Eisner or Adolf Hitler'.[21] Where then is the borderline between a type of charismatic rule which guarantees freedom within a democratic social order, and that which may result in the emergence of a totalitarian or quasi-totalitarian regime? Weber's political sociology is so designed that this question must be left unanswered. Some authors, for instance Arthur Schlesinger Jr., have suggested that the concept of "charisma' should therefore be discarded.[22] Others, in particular Karl Löwenstein, have attempted to modify Weber's concept of 'charismatic leadership' in such a way, as to make up for its deficiencies in this respect.[23] Carl Joachim Friedrich attempts to find an alternative solution. He resorts to the original religious meaning of 'charisma' and on this basis he suggests a differentiation between types of leadership, namely: 'democratic leadership' and 'ideological leadership'. According to Friedrich, Roosevelt and Churchill are outstanding examples of the former type, whereas 'ideological leadership' – which may operate both in a democratic as well as in a totalitarian society – applies primarily to party leaders.[24] It is debatable whether much is gained from such a distinction which is, incidentally, strongly biased in favour of pragmatic rather than ideological politics. For what is the difference between what Friedrich calls the personal and inspirational character of Theodore

Roosevelt's leadership and the kind of leadership which Max Weber had in mind when he called Gladstone a 'plebiscitarian dictator'? The irrational nature of their appeal to the masses is not substantially different from that of ideological leaders of a more or less totalitarian brand. Little is gained by giving them different labels.

There is perhaps another approach to the problem which might help to solve the puzzle of whether charismatic leadership is compatible with a democratic system. The essential weakness in Weber's concept of 'charismatic leadership' is not so much the irrational quality of charisma, although this is certainly of no small importance, but rather the notion that charisma not only qualifies a personality as a leader, but that it simultaneously legitimizes his authority, thus, at least indirectly, entitling him to unrestricted obedience from his followers. As long as the power of charisma is unimpaired by failure or defeat it is, for those who believe in it, a duty to obey the bearer of it. Unfortunately Weber did not distinguish sufficiently clearly between 'charismatic leadership' and 'charismatic domination', and from this omission result some of the problems mentioned above. For although it is quite feasible to accept the concept of 'charisma' in a formal sense as a criterion of leadership even in democratic systems, this surely has nothing to do with their legitimacy. Weber's opinion that in 'leadership democracies' authority rests only with the leaders and is, in fact, legitimized by their personal charisma although it is formally derived from the consent of the 'governed' (an interpretation of democracy, which he also put forward in his famous debate with Ludendorff in 1919)[25] was open to political abuse. When he argued that it is the charismatic qualification of leaders which matters whereas the democratic institutions are a mere functional machinery in their hands, he overstated his own case and came dangerously close to the 'Führerprinzip', the Fascist leadership principle.

Yet one should bear in mind that Max Weber developed his theory of the 'three pure types of legitimate domination' at a historical juncture, and with a historical perspective in mind, which was very different from our own. He did not envisage the possible rise of Fascist or other totalitarian regimes which, in fact, can be much better described as a combination of charismatic rule with bureaucratic techniques, than 'plebiscitarian democracy'. He was haunted by the prospect of a steady growth of the bureaucratic structures which was likely to put all individual freedom more and more in jeopardy. He considered stagnation and ossification the real dangers of his age, rather than charismatic break-throughs. In his opinion, the fatal decline of dynamism and mobility in politics could be cured only by one antidote, namely 'charismatic leadership'. Charismatic leaders had to check the aspirations of the bureaucracy. They had to break up its deadly rule of routine by their unique capacity to set new goals and to open up new paths in societies hampered by political stagnation and bureaucratic routine. It was up to them to keep the 'open society' open against the inhuman forces of bureaucratization. This could be achieved best within those democratic systems which allowed genuinely qualified politicians to realize their personal political conceptions with the techniques of both a 'positive' demagogy and efficient party machines. Parliamentary institutions on the other hand acted as a safeguard against the routinization of their charismatic qualities. For otherwise they might be tempted to turn to the techniques of manipulation and oppression instead of employing the legitimate means of persuasion and agitation, within a constitutional framework, which guarantees a maximum of free competition for leadership and power.

Notes

1. It is almost impossible to translate the German term *Herrschaft* to English. Differing from Roth and Wittich, the editors of the English edition of *Wirtschaft und Gesellschaft* we decided, after much consideration, to use the term 'domination' throughout as the most appropriate, in accordance with Raymond Aron and W. G. Runciman. The term 'authority' used by Roth and Wittich alternating with the term 'domination' is much too narrow, in so far as it refers primarily to the position of the actual person, or persons, in power. The compromise of Roth and Wittich, moreover, has the disadvantage that it obscures the almost rigid nature, as well as the meticulous symmetry, of Weber's systematization. It must be admitted that Weber tended to couch the problems of domination and rulership in a personalistic form, as is shown below; in this respect, the term 'authority' is, indeed, appropriate. On the other hand the theory of the 'Three Pure Types of Legitimate Domination' is meant to encompass political systems in their entirety and their respective ideological foundations, rather than the problem of the governmental authority only. For a long time we thought 'rule' to be the best term, as it does not quite carry the somewhat austere connotations of the word 'domination '. Yet it is also too narrow, covering only the activity of governing, although it is admirably suited to rendering correctly the relationship between the ruler (*Herrscher*) and the ruled (*die Beherrschten*). There is, unfortunately, no proper English cognate of 'domination' which is equivalent to the word *Herrscher* (ruler). On the other hand the term 'domination' comes closest to the somewhat authoritarian connotation which the word *Herrschaft* has in German, and it is a derivation from the Latin term *dominus* which is a perfect equivalent to the German term *Herrscher*. The linguistic difficulties raised here unfortunately do not allow us a completely satisfactory rendering in English of Weber's meticulous, almost pedantic, systematization of the 'three pure types'. For this reason at times the respective German term has been added in brackets.
2. For a discussion of the different versions of the theory of 'The Three Pure Types of Legitimate Domination' see above, p. 16f.
3. *WuG*, Vol. 1, pp. 122ff. (*EaS*, Vol. 1, pp. 212ff.).
4. The graph is intended to give a full picture of Weber's theory of the 'three pure types of legitimate domination'. To some degree it is a synthesis of all versions found in Weber's work. Cf. above p. 16f.
5. Bendix, p. 326.
6. Cf. below p. 106f. The author is indebted to Walter Kaufmann, *Nietzsche, Philosopher, Psychologist, Antichrist*, 1956, for an enlightening interpretation of Nietzsche on these lines.
7. Cf. *WuG*, Vol, 2, p. 735, and p. 757f. where Weber points out that the autonomous city states of northern Europe emerged from the political association of citizens, disregarding

and in opposition to the 'legitimate' authorities – the latter being, as a rule, the Emperor, a prince or an ecclesiastical potentate. This gives support to the conclusion given above which corresponds with the findings of recent research in medieval constitutional history.

8. *WuG*, Vol. 1, p. 28 (*EaS*, Vol. 1, p. 53). Roth's trans. slightly modified by the author. Cf. also *WuG*, Vol. 1, p. 122 (*EaS*, Vol. 1, p. 212).

9. Ibid., p. 29 (*EaS*, Vol. 1, p. 53; trans. by the author, differs from Roth's).

10. Cf. *WuG*, Vol. 1, p. 153: 'Grundlage *jeder* Herrschaft, also *jeder* Fügsamkeit, ist ein *Glauben*: "Prestige"-Glauben zugunsten des oder der Herrschenden.' This is trans. by Roth, *EaS*, Vol. 1, p. 263, as follows: 'In general it should be kept clearly in mind that the basis of every authority, and correspondingly of every kind of willingness to obey, is a *belief*, a belief by virtue of which persons exercising authority are lent prestige'. 'Prestige', however, is always largely dependent on the success of the rulers; hence it will not survive any substantial failure.

11. This solution was suggested by Adolf Arndt at the Soziologentag in Heidelberg 1964, (Cf. Stammer, p. 130), yet it does not hold water, because Weber did not mean that 'instrumentally-rational legal rule' cannot go together with elements of 'charismatic rule', or 'traditional rule'. Arndt's argument would be valid only on the premise that the 'three pure types of legitimate domination' are incompatible with one another.

12. This was undertaken recently by Martin E. Spencer, 'Weber on Legitimate Norms and Authority', *British Journal of Sociology*, Vol. 21, 1970, pp. 123ff., in a not very illuminating manner. For Spencer fails to pay sufficient attention to the universal scope of Weber's theory of the 'three pure types of legitimate domination', and also does not discuss Weber's claim that this systematization was meant to be comprehensive, both in time, *and* in substance. It is even more irritating to see that Spencer does not take into account that Weber *has* given some thought to the sub-type of 'value-oriented legality', yet he did not think it a viable form of legitimacy in modern industrial societies. Spencer's suggestion that a fourth type called 'value-rational authority' ought to be added, is hence rather naive, and surely is not on the same level as that on which Weber discussed these difficult questions. For a far more substantial, although not always consistent, discussion of the issue in question see Karl Löwenstein, *Max Webers staatspolitische Auffassungen in der Sicht unserer Zeit*, Frankfurt, Bonn, 1965 (English trans.: *Max Weber's Political Ideas in the Perspective of our Time*, 1966), pp. 71ff.

13. Quoted in Mommsen, *Max Weber*, p. 392.

14. *WuG*, Vol. 1, p. 157 (author's trans.). Cf. *EaS*, Vol. 1, p. 269.

15. *PS*, p. 535 (Gerth, p. 106).

16. Ibid., p. 535 (Gerth, p. 107).

17. Ibid., p. 544. (Cf. Gerth, p. 113.)

18. For a detailed analysis of Max Weber's concept of 'leader democracy' see W. J. Mommsen, 'Zum Begriff der plebiszitären Führerdemokratie bei Max Weber', *Kölner Zeitschrift für Soziologie und Sozialpsychologie*, Vol. 15, 1965, pp. 295ff.

19. *WuG*, Vol. 1, p. 156 (author's trans.; cf. *EaS*, Vol. 1, p. 268).

20. *WuG*, Vol. 1, p. 157 (*EaS*, Vol. 1, p. 269).

21. Cf. Arnold Bergstraesser, 'Max Weber's akademische Antrittsrede', *Vierteljahreshefte für Zeitgeschichte*, Vol. 5, 1957, p. 209.

22. Arthur Schlesinger, 'Democracy and Heroic Leadership in the Twentieth Century' (paper read at the Congress of Cultural Freedom, Berlin, June 1960) argues that 'Weber's typology neither derives from nor applies to a study of democratic society . . .' Cf. Karl Joachim Friedrich, 'Political Leadership and the Problem of Charismatic Power', *Journal of Politics*, Vol. 23, 1961, p. 16, note 24.

23. Cf. Karl Löwenstein, op. cit., pp. 71ff. Löwenstein objects in particular to the identification of 'plebiscitarian' and 'cesarist' rule by Weber.

24. Friedrich, op. cit., pp. 17ff.

25. Cf. *Lebensbild*, pp. 702f.

CHAPTER 5

A Liberal in Despair

Talcott Parsons pointed out some years ago that Max Weber stood at a very crucial juncture in the development of Western civilization.[1] Indeed, his scholarly work as well as his political role seems to mark a new departure in the realm of ideas just as much as in political thought, although perhaps not exactly in the way Talcott Parsons was inclined to see it: that is, that 'Weber heralded the end of Ideology'.[2] It may be useful to point out that Max Weber wrote his major works in a time of substantial change in the political as well as in the intellectual sphere. By the turn of the century politics were profoundly influenced by a popular nationalism which the ruling classes did not know how to direct to useful ends. The First World War resulted in the breakdown of the traditional European order which had rested on a sort of compromise between the traditional ruling classes and the middle classes, while the working classes for the most part had still not been integrated into the political system at all. In the last resort the recourse to war had been little more than a desperate attempt to placate the new nationalism of the middle classes, since all traditionalist values seemed to have lost their hold on the people at large.

It was in this period that Weber wrote most of his works, in a mood of almost complete frustration over German politics. Weber had realized long before the outbreak of the First World War that he was living in a society which rested on rather shaky foundations. He, for one, was well aware of the fact that a revaluation of many of the values on which the political as well as the social system were based was already well under way, although few people realized it at the time. Max Weber had been brought up in the ideological atmosphere of German bourgeois Liberalism. His father had been a National Liberal politician who had played an important role in the inner circle of the leaders of the National Liberal Party in Berlin. The grandeur of the German Empire rather than ideas about constitutional rule and the like, was the prevailing political value in this circle. A secularized Protestantism and a stern morality of an almost puritan cast were also important factors in Weber's intellectual upbringing. On the other hand Weber's intellectual development was strongly influenced by the German Idealist tradition, with its strong emphasis on the autonomous personality.

His political views were originally in line for the most part with the ideas of German National Liberalism which was, above all, strongly nationalist, and which staunchly admired the political genius of Bismarck. German Liberalism was never substantially influenced by the Western European doctrine of the natural rights of man; it was dominated rather by the idea that the autonomy of the individual must be safeguarded in society and politics alike, and that for this reason the educated classes should have a share in legislative matters, as they were bound to interfere with their social and economic activities. The freedom of the individual from undue interference by the state was of more concern than his having a proper share in the process of actual decision making. For this reason German Liberalism never pushed its political claims further than requesting constitutional rule and local self-government.

The individualistic tradition of German Liberalism was a strong influence on Max Weber. For him the principle of the free initiative of the individual was the very core of the Liberal creed. His individualistic views were corroborated and, indeed, further strengthened by the influence of Nietzsche, whose philosophy emphasizes the role of the creative individual in intellectual life as well as in the social and political spheres. Weber always maintained that every social order should be so designed as to give maximum opportunity to individuals to act on their own free initiative. He advocated the intervention of the state only where the situation would no longer allow this. This was particularly the case in the field of industrial relations where the balance of power, in Weber's opinion, had been changed altogether to the disadvantage of the working classes. The state, he argued, should step in and introduce appropriate legislation in order to restore the balance, and thus make it possible for the workers to fight with the entrepreneurs over their working conditions on an equal footing.

This is, however, just one indication of the difficulties of traditional Liberalism at a time when what we now would call monopoly capitalism and huge bureaucracies were to become more and more dominant. Weber noted, with considerable apprehension, that the German middle classes were not capable of taking over the role of the predominant political class from the declining nobility and were thus unable to fulfil the mission which seemed to be assigned to them by history.

This was partly due to objective factors. As a consequence of the advance of industrialization the bourgeois classes everywhere tended to disintegrate politically as well as socially. The rapidly growing diversity of the structure of incomes was bound to destroy the relative homogeneity which the middle classes had enjoyed in the earlier nineteenth century, and it also undermined their bourgeois ethos. In the German case, things were particularly bad in this respect. German Liberalism had split into a large number of rival groups which no longer agreed even on the most fundamental political issues. Politically German Liberalism by 1900 was in a state of permanent frustration; the Liberals had neither the political energies nor any chance to overcome the opposition of their political adversaries. Under pressure from the labour movement they were content if they could hold their own.

As is borne out by his famous 'Inaugural Lecture' at the University of Freiburg in 1895, Weber felt very strongly about this. To no small degree he identified himself personally with the destinies of German bourgeois Liberalism, calling himself explicitly 'a member of the bourgeois classes'.[3] He also shared the conviction of many Liberals of the time that they were *Epigonen*, as compared with the great generation which assisted Bismarck in founding the Empire.

He was deeply worried that German Liberalism was not in a position to take the political lead in German society, since, in his opinion, it was not equal to the historical tasks which it ought to fulfil. Furthermore, he realized that the traditional liberal ideology had lost much of its persuasive power in an emerging industrial society characterized by growing bureaucracies and industrial combinations. Also the time-honoured liberal idea that the power of the state should be restricted as much as possible, in order to allow society to develop along natural lines, seemed to Weber entirely inadequate in an age of power politics and Imperialism. He took up the opposite position, and spoke passionately in favour of a staunch policy of Imperialist expansion.[4] New Imperialist tasks would provide a rallying point for the nation at large, under a banner which at the same time stood for liberalization and modernization at home. It seems that in the late 1890s he adhered to the opinion that the bourgeois social and economic system was not likely to survive for long without the safety valve of commercial outlets and territorial possessions overseas – the more so, as further continuous economic growth was apparently dependent on the latter.[5]

The problem of how to adapt Liberal principles to the conditions of the emerging industrial society was, for Weber, of first-rate importance and just as much a political issue as a personal one. Gradually he came to realize more and more sharply how serious the situation was, in view of his conviction that the only creative factor in society is the free initiative of the individual personality. Around the turn of the century he was inclined to view the future with gloom. He feared that sooner or later the dynamic process of capitalist expansion would come to a halt, partly because there would be no more virgin lands offering the opportunity of further economic expansion, and partly because technology was not likely to advance at the same rate for ever. Already in his own day – according to his pessimistic outlook – some of the elements were being created which would eventually help to bring about a stagnant society of a bureaucratic nature which in some ways was likely to be similar to the conditions in the late Roman Empire. 'The bureaucratization of society will, according to all available knowledge, someday triumph over capitalism, in our civilization just as in ancient civilizations. In our civilization also the "anarchy of production" will be supplanted in due course by an economic and social system similar to that typical of the Late Roman Empire, and even more so of the "New Kingdom" in Egypt or the sway of the Ptolemies'.[6]

Weber pointed out on various occasions that it would be totally wrong to assume that capitalism had anything in common with modern democracy and with liberal ideals. In his opinion the opposite was true. The rise of capitalist industrialism was associated with the rise of ever more gigantic and powerful bureaucracies on all levels of social life, and he believed that this process would eventually bring about a thoroughly 'goal-oriented' type of society in which purely instrumental relationships would dominate social conduct everywhere. He couched his fears in forceful language which at times reminds us of the Jewish prophecies. He maintained that eventually rationalization and intellectualization – being the two most effective revolutionary forces in world history – would no longer permit individual creativity and personal values to play any significant role in social relations. At best sublime values would be allowed to survive in the retreat of complete privacy, while the social system would be completely dominated by purely instrumental (*zweckrationale*) social relationships, and interactions.

Weber doubted whether under the conditions being created by capitalism a free society of the liberal type was likely to survive for long. He maintained, contrary to the current belief, that capitalist development would in turn lead to a liberalization of authoritarian societies and that capitalism had nothing whatever in common with freedom and democracy (this referred to Tsarist Russia). Hence the vital question of his age was as follows: 'How are, under its rule' [i.e. capitalism], 'all these things' [that is to say, the rights of man, individual liberties, the freedom of the press and so forth] 'permanently possible?'[7] Once the current rapid expansion of capitalism had come to a halt, and the dynamism of capitalist competition had given way to bureaucratic techniques of regulating the economy, any society which was organized in accordance with liberal and democratic principles, was bound to collapse: 'In American "benevolent feudalism", in the German so-called "welfare institutions", in the Russian "factory system", everywhere the House of Serfdom is already at hand; we just have to wait until the diminishing speed of technological and economic progress, as well as the triumph of rents over profits, in connection with the exhaustion of all "free" regions and markets all over the world, will eventually push the masses into accepting the situation and moving into it'.[8] These bleak forecasts undoubtedly exaggerated the dangers to which the individualistic societies of the West were exposed by the rapid growth of capitalism and bureaucratic machineries – at any rate in the short run. Yet they demonstrate clearly how strongly Max Weber felt about the necessity to fight this trend, and to do everything in his power to defend the liberal social order of his day.

This conclusion is confirmed by an analysis of that part of Weber's work which, perhaps more than any other, helped to establish his worldwide reputation as one of the founding fathers of modern sociology; namely his studies on the *Protestant Ethic and the Rise of Capitalism*. Max Weber became interested in this topic somewhat accidentally, yet nonetheless his interest in it had much to do with his liberal, if not, his bourgeois convictions. By 1900 the idea that there must be a correlation between the rise of capitalism and religious beliefs had been very much in the air, and the thesis that the Protestants had played a considerable part in the early phases of the industrial revolution was harboured by many people. Furthermore, such an approach which attempted to trace particular significant historical developments back to religious beliefs, or to specific ideologies, was completely in line with the then dominant methodology of German history. Jellinek had just completed a study on the 'Origins of the *Rights of Man*' which maintained that these ideas had been first developed by the Levellers. Max Weber, it would seem, was convinced that the specific 'bourgeois virtues' – thriftiness, rational conduct of one's own business as well as one's own life, honesty in business as well as in personal life, willingness to work hard – were just as much of puritan origin; and he was therefore thoroughly dissatisfied with Sombart's theory regarding the origins of modern capitalism. In contrast to Sombart he maintained that the rise of modern industrial capitalism was due in no small degree to particular bourgeois values. And his attempt to prove his case was, at the same time, an attempt to state once again the significance of bourgeois values in world history as distinct from those of the aristocracy.

It is not possible in this context to go into the details of Weber's famous thesis with regard to the origins of capitalism. To this day it is the subject of heated controversy. I should like only to point out what was, in the context of Weber's thought, the core of his argument. He maintained that 'other-worldly value orientations' (*ausserweltliche Werthaltungen*) of an unusually stringent nature had induced the Puritans to organize their lives as well as their business activities on a thoroughly rational basis, thereby creating that type of social conduct which according to Weber is the necessary precondition for the development of modern industrial capitalism. The unending struggle of the Puritans to live up to specific 'other-worldly norms' – not just the lust for profit – induced them to concentrate all their energies as well as their savings on the production of industrial goods. They did so without paying any attention to the traditional habits and patterns of economic behaviour of their environment, and for this very reason a process of *world historical magnitude* was initiated which could eventually sustain itself.

At the bottom of all this lies a particular contention as to how far-reaching social change is likely to be effected in history. Weber argued that it is the 'value-oriented' actions of individuals, or, possibly, small groups of individuals, which bring social change about, and these actions are likely to be the more far reaching, the more the values, ideals, or normative principles in question stand out in contrast to social reality and the traditional patterns of social conduct given at the time. Or, to put this another way: it is the enormous tension between any given set of ultimate values on the one hand, and empirical reality on the other hand, which begets extraordinary social achievements. It is only by grasping far beyond the everyday reality that great inner-worldly achievements come about.

Weber's research on the sociology of the world religions was undertaken primarily in order to corroborate the findings of the 'Protestant Ethic' *ex negativo*. And, indeed, nothing similar to the religious attitude of the Puritans could be found elsewhere. Either these other beliefs advocated an 'other-worldly asceticism', that is to say, a thorough retreat from this world – which implied that they remained socially inactive – or they heralded the principle of thorough adjustment to the given social order rather than putting up normative demands which would have required a line of social conduct which might lead to conflicts with, and hence, alterations of, the given social order. It is only in ancient Judaism that Weber discovered something which could be said to have had similar effects on the believers as the Puritan dogma, namely the charisma of the prophets.

Weber observed that the extreme demands of the prophets on the Jewish people had in many cases affected a sort of rationalization of conduct similar to the Puritan one. The prophets, it would seem, also induced their followers to subject their personal lives to the iron law of rational conduct designed to bring about maximum efficiency. This discovery had a tremendous effect on the further development of Weber's scholarly work. Charismatic leadership follows exactly the same pattern of social conduct as Puritanism, in so far as groups of followers are willing to make the values of the charismatic leader their own, and to do everything in their power to reconstruct social reality in accordance with them. The concept of charisma, then, must be considered as a more general version of Weber's fundamental contention that it is the value-oriented action of individuals who, by grasping for something far beyond their reach for 'other-worldly' and not day-to-day reasons, bring such enormous energies to bear on social reality that the course of events is given a new direction, or in other words, that the social order is revolutionized. Charisma emerges as the only creative revolutionary force in history, and, in a way, it is the only form in which the individual personality is capable of sensibly influencing the course of events in an age of ever more powerful bureaucracies.

The quest for charismatic leaders consequently seems to offer a solution, however partial, to the problems which Weber faced. Yet this is just one side of the coin. Weber assumed that the creative force or charisma was doomed, at least in the long run, in view of the seemingly irresistible advance of routinization, rationalization and bureaucratization. Secondly, Weber strongly objected to taking refuge in what might have been an easy escape from the harsh conclusions of his own analysis, by joining forces outright with the anti-rationalist movement which was quite strong in the first decades of the twentieth century. He, for one, would have nothing in common with Stefan George and his personality cult, or with Spengler's Germanic myths.

Weber's halfway, and perhaps somewhat ambiguous, position comes to the fore particularly in his attitude towards capitalism itself. Capitalism had been, according to Weber, the offspring of the type of individualistic social conduct which he identified with the liberal bourgeois ethos, yet on the other hand capitalism was the decisive social force which fostered the growth of bureaucracies and purely instrumental, or, in Weber's own terms, 'goal-oriented' types of social interaction, to the lasting detriment of all forms of individual creative social activities. Weber's indecision is reflected in his attitude to two other social philosophies which had profoundly influenced his own thinking, namely Karl Marx and Friedrich Nietzsche. The influence of Nietzsche on Max Weber has so far not been given adequate consideration. Weber was, however, strongly influenced by Nietzsche's aristocratic philosophy, and his own stand in regard to the question of ultimate values cannot be understood properly without reference to Nietzsche.[9] Weber is said to have remarked late in his life to one of his students: 'The honesty of a scholar of our day, and even more of a philosopher of our day can be judged on the grounds of how he defines his relationship to Nietzsche and Marx. He who denies that he would have been unable to achieve the most important parts of his own work without the work of both of them, belies himself just as much as the others. The world in which we live as intellectual beings, bears largely the imprint of Marx and Nietzsche'.[10]

What is important in our context is that both Nietzsche and Marx had spoken up passionately against the sort of society which was being created by capitalist industrialism; a society which seemed to both to be an altogether inhumane one. Admittedly Marx had accepted capitalism as a necessary transitional social formation, eventually to be supplanted by a communist society which would put things right again. Nietzsche, on the other hand, did not share Marx's optimistic outlook. He violently denounced the emerging industrial order as the gravedigger of a sublime culture created and sustained by a few great individuals who were far superior to the masses. Nietzsche maintained that the ultimate cause of all this had been the 'miserabilistic ethic' of Christianity, and he heralded with some relief the revaluation of all values – a course of events which would possibly pave the way for the eventual rise of a new social order of a thoroughly aristocratic nature, in which human beings in the full sense of the word could again emerge.

Max Weber worked out his own position, paying due consideration to these two altogether contradictory social philosophies, and he eventually arrived at what might be called a dialectal standpoint with regard to both. As we have already pointed out, he bluntly rejected the Marxist theory of historical development, which he considered sheer nonsense, in as much as it claimed to be based on scientific principles.[11] Yet at the same time he accepted it, although seemingly without much enthusiasm, as an important working hypothesis for social science. His own research into the origins of capitalism would indicate that at least in the initial stages of its emergence ideal factors, in particular religious convictions, had played a decisive, if not all important role; and hence he rejected Marx's theory of the Überbau. As is borne out by all his sociological work, Weber was firmly convinced that value attitudes as well as social expectations resulting from particular cultural traditions are just as important as material interests. Weber did not share Marx's conviction that the contradictions of capitalist society could be done away with by a proletarian revolution which abolished the private appropriation of the means of production. He did not think that socialism offered a solution to the pressing problems which mankind was confronted with. He was firmly convinced – and I think that in this respect history since then has been on his side – that it is not capitalism and the capitalist pattern of the distribution of property which was putting a humane order of things in jeopardy, but rather the growth of bureaucracies. In view of this a nationalization of the means of production did not alter things in the least; far from emancipating the working classes from the status of 'alienation', it would make it worse. For all socialist policies were, in his opinion, bound to foster bureaucratization, and hence to reinforce the tendencies towards an ossification of society.[12]

There was just one type of socialism which Weber was prepared to take seriously, the Utopian, almost anarchist, socialism of the Russian *émigrés* with whom he entertained close connexions in Heidelberg before and during the First World War. As a purely moralist conviction which did not take account of the chances of a realization at all – that is to say, on *gesinnungsethische* grounds – he could digest, and even give serious consideration to the idea of socialism, yet he loathed it in the pseudo-scientific version of orthodox Marxism.

With regard to Nietzsche the balance sheet seems to be more positive. There is no doubt that the impact of Nietzsche's individualistic nihilism on Weber's thought had been strong indeed. With Nietzsche originates what is perhaps one of the key concepts of Weber's personal creed, the concept of *intellektuelle Redlichkeit* (intellectual honesty). Some of Nietzsche's key arguments turn up repeatedly in Weber's sociology of world religions, although not always unopposed.[13] Weber's contention that every individual has to choose his own values, and to put them to the proof in the way in which he conducts his own life, is deeply indebted to Nietzsche's philosophy. It is, however, more important to note that Weber was strongly affected by Nietzsche's prognosis that Western civilization was on the decline, and that all modern mass movements had dangerous levelling consequences. It is true that Weber did not accept all of this, yet even so he was undoubtedly influenced by Nietzsche's message that it is the great personalities who make up the essence of history. However, he refused to go all the way with Nietzsche. He strongly objected to Nietzsche's aristocratic contempt of the masses. In his opinion the great personality is great only in so far as it goes with the masses, not against them. Also he would not have anything to do with the vulgar Nietzscheanism of his contemporaries.

Actually Weber worked out a sort of compromise between Nietzsche's intellectual aristocratism and his own liberal convictions. To put it another way, he tried to harmonize the doctrine of the Levellers with the message of Nietzsche, as far as this was possible. At the same time he combined Marx's findings and his own discoveries as to the nature of bureaucratization and rationalization with Nietzsche's prognosis that the 'last men' on this earth must eventually give way to a mass of faceless men incapable of displaying any higher, humane interests.

In a famous passage in the Introduction to the *Wirtschaftsethik der Weltreligionen*, which was written fairly late in his life, Weber attempted to formulate his own position, as deviating from Marx, without disowning him altogether: 'Interests (material and ideal ones), not ideas, determine the actions of men directly. The *Weltbilder* that were created by "ideas", however, very often were the switchmen who determined the lines alongside which the dynamism of interests pushed human action onwards'.[14]

'Ideal interests' are, in Weber's opinion, by no means merely ideologies; they are rather a social force in their own right; and Weber, indeed, held the notion that this is the way in which creative individual action makes itself felt in the course of history. However, he was careful to avoid taking up a naive idealist position; on the contrary, he made it quite clear that most men are guided in their social conduct and their social activities by interests of various kinds, which in turn are largely determined by material considerations. Yet at the same time he strongly adhered to the opinion that ideas *can* change the course of events, if only indirectly, by influencing the intellectual outlook and consequently the social expectations of men. It is at this point that Weber follows Nietzsche's contention that it is the duty of great individuals to set forth values and goals for the people at large. On the other hand, Weber accepted Marx's interpretation that by and large social processes are directed, and, indeed, propelled forward by the 'dynamism of material interests'. He did not think, however, that in this respect the form of the appropriation of the means of production was of decisive importance, although he himself argued that only a system of private ownership could achieve a maximum of formal rationality and, hence, at least to some degree, a maximum of efficiency. In his opinion, it was not the workers' deprivation of the means of production which was the most significant feature of modern industrial capitalism – this element it had, in fact, in common with many previous civilizations – but the continuous advance of ever more bureaucratic forms of social organizations, primarily in the economic, but of necessity also in the political field, in order to maximize production, profits, and the supply of goods to an ever widening, yet at the same time more competitive market. Modern capitalism was, as a matter of fact, affiliated with bureaucratization and rationalization in so many ways that the dynamism of the capitalist process inevitably resulted in a steady growth of more and more gigantic bureaucratic structures. From the point of view of Weber's individualistic philosophy it was the latter factor, which mattered above all, and what he was most concerned about.

It is, therefore, by no means surprising, and in fact completely in line with Weber's most fundamental assumptions about the role of man in history that in *Wirtschaft und Gesellschaft* there emerge two sets of forces that bring about social change, namely 'other-worldly', (and very often religious) beliefs on the one hand, and rationalization, routinization and bureaucratization on the other hand. While the latter forces work anonymously, propelled by material interests, the former are implemented only by men who are willing to give themselves up completely to these beliefs, and to rationalize their lives so as to achieve a maximum effect with regard to the basic values they adhere to. Weber, as it were, gradually came round to the assumption that this could be initiated, at least in modern societies, only by charismatic leadership. Hence the concept of charisma – which Weber had conceived originally as applying predominantly to earlier forms of civilizations – eventually emerged as a key concept in his sociology, as well as in his political theory, being the only viable counterpart of bureaucracy.

It is at this point that one may object on the grounds that Weber believed in value neutrality, and in his main work *Wirtschaft und Gesellschaft* tried hard to abstain from all value judgements. There can be no doubt that the abstention from value judgements was one of the basic principles of Weber's work. And, indeed, many empirical social scientists have labelled Max Weber as one of their forefathers because of his endeavours to develop a kind of general theory of social action which was, or rather claimed to be, free of so-called value judgements. I do not want to raise the point whether Max Weber actually succeeded in this; I would like to point out, however, that there are important differences between Weber's idea of 'abstention from value judgements' and the position of contemporary empirical social science. The latter attempts to eliminate everything which may be called values in a traditional language, in order to be able to formulate general theories that can be used to explain as well as to predict social processes of various kinds. Weber admittedly did take some steps in this direction, but he never considered this to be an ultimate objective of the social sciences. He rather headed for something substantially different. He worked hard to eliminate all value judgements, not so much in order to get rid of value judgements as such altogether, but rather to enable the individual or groups of individuals to bring them to bear all the more powerfully on a given social context and a given situation.

This is clearly brought out by the history of Weber's own belief in *Werturteilsfreiheit*. As early as 1895 he had strongly argued in his famous "Inaugural Lecture" at Freiburg that science can never establish nor prove the validity of any values, yet he did this in order to make clear beyond doubt that the ideas of nationality and the preservation of the nation state by all suitable means deserved preference to the supposedly well-established principle of maximum productivity, with regard to the economic and political conditions of the areas in Eastern Prussia. And Simey has shown that much the same kind of motives induced Weber to launch the famous debate on value neutrality in the *Verein für Socialpolitik* in 1913.[15] For many years Weber and his brother Alfred had challenged the conservative course of Schmoller, raising numerous political issues – for instance, the attitude of heavy industry towards social policy, the issue of parliamentary versus bureaucratic government, and many others – all without any doubt involving value judgements. Now all of a sudden Weber asked his adversaries to abstain from all value judgements in their scholarly work. This, as it were, seemed somewhat odd to the majority of the members of the

Verein für Socialpolitik. What Weber was really after was to put an end to the mixture of social science and conservative politics which was represented by Schmoller and his school, because social science of such a kind favoured in its effects the existing semi-bureaucratic type of government in Germany. By not clearly distinguishing between value judgements and the findings of empirical research, both, argued Max Weber, were to suffer; a clear-cut choice between different sets of values, something which is the essence of all politics as well as of social reform, would be made almost impossible.

Rather than present value judgements in a scientific drapery of whatever kind, the social sciences should make clear which value options lie behind the various controversial issues in modern society, and enable people to make the right choices in view of their own values – instead of suggesting to them in a semi-authoritarian way quasi-objective solutions of social problems. It was, according to Weber, the most sublime, and most essential task of all social science, to make people aware of their own values, or their value preferences, and to make them face the inevitable conflict of values which occurs in any given concrete situation. Lastly, science should help them to decide rationally what to do, and this, of course, meant taking all foreseeable consequences into account. This rather rigid theory implied, incidentally, a particular kind of formal ethics. It rested, as it were, on the assumption that it is only the individual who, in the pre-rational sphere of the personality, can decide on value issues, and that in doing this he chooses his own destiny.

Weber's sociological work was, as regards its final intentions, so designed as to fulfil this very task. It should enable people to choose rationally between different sets of values in any given situation, which required the making of decisions. It was intended not only to provide casual explanations for various kinds of social actions; but it was supposed to make choices between different sets of values no longer a matter of mere emotional reactions or of guesswork, but of rational deliberation conducted in view of the foreseeable results, as a responsible operation.

For that very reason Weber also stuck to a strictly individualistic methodology in social science. Although he spoke constantly in his sociology of social groups of all kinds, classes, castes, parties, and the like, he was rigidly opposed to any sociology working on collectivist principles. 'The individual is, even if viewed from the point of view of larger social units, the only embodiment of meaningful behaviour.)[16] In March 1920, a few months before his death, Max Weber wrote to Liefmann: 'Sociology can be done only by taking its starting point in the actions of the individual or individuals – they may be few or many – or, to put it in another way: in a strictly "individualistic" manner'.[17]

It must be admitted, however, that Weber himself attempted to fore-stall any argument which would try to establish a formal link between his methodological views and his personal convictions. 'It is a tremendous misunderstanding to think that an "individualistic" *method* should involve what is in any conceivable sense an individualistic system of values'.[18] This may well be true, yet even so it would seem that in view of the ultimate goal assigned by Weber to the social sciences – that is, to help the individual to lead a rational life fully in line with his values – he was bound to take this position. For in order to be able to do so, the social sciences must take into account the value-oriented motives of individual persons or groups, and attempt to evaluate their actions in view of their own objectives and values. It is for this reason that Weber could not dispose of the method of *Verstehen*, for only in this way could one establish links between actual social processes and the value assumptions of particular individuals or groups, which then resulted in a better comprehension of the values involved, as well as the inevitable conflict between the latter.

For the personality, in Weber's own understanding, it was vital to be as fully aware as possible of the conflicts between different sets of values, for as he occasionally put it, 'its essence lies in the constancy of its inner relationship to specific ultimate "values" and "life-meanings"' that determine his actions, and have a rationalizing effect on his social conduct in all spheres of life.[19]

Here the two ends of Weber's thought come together again. His scholarly work was, to a substantial degree intended to make it possible for personalities to live in the modern world without giving themselves up to irrational faiths, myths or prophecies. On the other hand he could not but concede that all forms of individualistic, value-oriented conduct were universally on the retreat. In fact, Weber gradually abandoned his original position which had placed side by side the types of 'value-oriented conduct – the Puritan inner-worldly asceticism being the most conspicuous case for this – and 'goal-oriented' rational conduct. More and more he was inclined to think that, under the conditions of modern bureaucratic societies, charisma was the only force which could possibly check the advance of routinization and purely instrumental social institutions. He eventually subsumed all social activity which could be described as emanating from individual initiative under the concept of charisma. Charisma was described by him as the only creative force in history; a force which, unlike the forces of rationalization and routinization, revolutionizes men from the inside out, and which by doing so is capable of mobilizing social energies of such a magnitude that it becomes possible to break through the confines of a rationalized world and to impart a new direction to the course of events. History is, from Weber's individualistic point of view, in the last resort, more or less identical with what he occasionally called 'the variegated struggle between disciplinization and individual charisma'.[20]

With regard to the eventual outcome of this eternal struggle, which may as well be defined as an eternal strife between two types of human beings, the *Ordnungsmenschen* and the *Kulturmenschen* Weber was extremely pessimistic: 'When the rationalization of the means of satisfaction of all political as well as all social needs will be completed, disciplinization as a universal phenomenon will make irresistible headway in every sphere of human life. Consequently charisma and all individually oriented forms of social action will have less and less importance'.[21] Weber was not, however, willing simply to resign himself to this. In what has been aptly described as a sort of heroic pessimism he resorted to a series of fairly radical measures which were designed to keep the 'open society' of his day 'open', as long as there was any point in doing so. It is at this point that Max Weber reveals himself as a Liberal in despair. For the moment there were no prophets around, and it was futile to do nothing while waiting for them to appear.[22] Rather one should do everything possible to keep society as dynamic as possible.

For this reason there ought to be a permanent struggle between nation states just as between different values, rather than eternal peace and weak compromise, possibly even forced upon the world by the rule of a universal power state; in this respect the example of the late Roman Empire was anything but encouraging. In internal politics also there ought to be as much dynamism as possible, and consequently open struggle and conflict between the various groups and classes – although the legal framework of the parliamentary democracy was to ensure that physical violence was reduced to a minimum.

Yet above all there ought to be a dynamic leadership which was both competent and imaginative. It is for this reason that Weber eventually advocated the 'plebiscitarian leader-democracy', in contrast to the various types of what he called 'democracies without leadership' (*führerlose Demokratien*), which adhere to the principle of the minimization of domination of man over man.[23] In sociological terms Weber defined plebiscitarian democracy – being 'the most important type of *"Führerdemokratie"*' – as a special version of charismatic domination which derives its legitimacy formally from the consent of the governed, yet in fact from their emotional devotion to the plebiscitarian leader.[24] In this system of government the plebiscitarian leader is entitled to be in absolute command not only of the administrative machinery, but the party organization – the party machine – as well; he can also request unreserved obedience on behalf of his followers as long as he is in power, whatever their own convictions may be. Max Weber was, of course, aware of the dangers inherent in this kind of highly emotional rule, yet in his opinion this disadvantage was offset by the fact that thereby maximum efficiency, and at the same time, a maximum degree of political dynamism would be ensured. Or to put it in a different way: there ought to be as powerful a rule as possible by responsible charismatic leaders, and at the same time effective control of their doings by rival leaders, in order to guarantee a maximum of mobility in politics and society, and hence a maximum opportunity for individual creativity on the political level.

In taking such a position Max Weber was about to abandon the platform of traditional liberalism, in particular the traditional concept of a liberal-democratic order.[25] This is the case in particular with regard to the concept of parliamentary democracy which he defined as being little more than a system of selecting qualified political leaders. Yet he assumed that there was no other choice left in view of the secular trends in society and politics alike.

Did Max Weber, we may ask again, really herald the 'end of ideologies'? Definitely not in the sense which Parsons had in mind in 1964, namely that empirical sociology would have to take over in order to solve those social problems which the traditional scholarly disciplines ridden by ideologies of all sorts, had failed to do. In ossified societies which are dominated through and through by bureaucratic institutions, ideologies would indeed be stripped of all importance. Max Weber, however, did not envisage anything of this kind in the near future, as is borne out by his famous public lecture 'Science as a Vocation'. He admitted that the 'disenchantment of the world' would inevitably continue, but this would not mean that all struggle for the realization of ultimate values was to come to an end, at least not in the immediate future. He rather maintained that in the time ahead social conflicts were likely to become more intense than ever before. He argued, in words which are very close to Nietzsche's, that after a period of relative tranquillity, which was to no small extent due to the tranquillizing influence of Christianity, 'the old plurality of Gods ascend from their graves, they are disenchanted and hence take the form of impersonal forces. They strive to gain power over our lives, and again they resume their eternal struggle with one another'.[26] Looking back after fifty years this prognosis has come to be much more accurate than Max Weber himself had assumed in his own lifetime.

Notes

1. Stammer, p. 40.
2. Ibid., p. 63.
3. *PS*, p. 20: 'Ich bin ein Mitglied der bürgerlichen Klassen, fühle mich als solches und bin erzogen in ihren Anschauungen und Idealen'.
4. Cf. above, pp. 41ff.

5. For a detailed analysis of this issue see Mommsen, *Max Weber*, pp. 54ff., and idem in Stammer, pp. 13off.
6. *Gesammelte Aufsätze zur Sozial- und Wirtschaftsgeschichte*, p. 277 (author's trans.).
7. *PS*, p. 64.
8. Ibid., p. 63.
9. I should like to refer here to Mommsen, *Universalgeschichtliches Denken*, pp. 571ff., and to Eugene Fleischmann, 'De Weber à Nietzsche', *Archives Européennes de Sociologie*, vol. 5, 1964, pp. 190ff. Fleischmann, however, overestimates the influence of Nietzsche on Weber a great deal. A forthcoming Harvard doctoral dissertation by Robert Eden, 'Political Leadership and Philosophic Praxis: A Study of Weber and Nietzsche', will throw new light on this problem.
10. Cf. Eduard Baumgarten, *Max Weber. Werk und Person*, Tübingen, 1964, pp. 554ff., note 1 (author's trans.). The authenticity of this statement is, however, somewhat dubious.
11. CL above, pp. 50ff.
12. A lengthier exposition of this point is to be found above, pp. 57ff.
13. See on this point the arguments of Jacob Taubes, in Stammer, pp. 222ff.
14. *RS*, Vol. 1, p. 252 (author's trans.).
15. Cf. T. S. Simey, 'Max Weber: Man of Affairs or Theoretical Sociologist?', *The Sociological Review*, Vol. 14, 1966, pp. 303ff.
16. *WL*, p. 439. Cf. *WuG*, Vol. 1, pp. 7f.
17. Letter to Robert Liefmann, 9 March 1920, quoted in J. Mommsen, *Universalgeschichtliches Denken*, p. 576f., note 57 (author's trans.).
18. *WuG*, Vol. 1, p. 9 (*EaS*, Vol. 1, p. 18).
19. *WL*, p. 132.
20. *WuG*, Vol. 2, p. 691 (author's trans.). Cf. *EaS*, Vol. 3, p. 1150.
21. Ibid., p. 695 (author's trans.). Cf. *EaS*, Vol. 3, p. 1156.
22. For Weber's condemnation of such attitudes see his famous public lecture 'Wissenschaft als Beruf', *WL*, p. 609f.
23. A systematic treatment of this aspect of Weber's political theory will be found in Mommsen, *Plebiszitäre Führerdemokratie*.
24. Above we have attempted a precise location of the type of 'plebiscitarian democracy' within Weber's systematization of the 'Three Types of Legitimate Domination', pp. 87ff.
25. This issue is fully discussed, though from a somewhat more dogmatic viewpoint than I would entertain nowadays, in Mommsen, *Max Weber*. The arguments put forward there initiated a heated controversy that has not yet come to an end. Some authors, however, would seem to close their eyes to the serious problems involved in a theory of democracy that relies to a substantial degree on the concept of charisma. See, for instance, Anthony Giddens, *Political Thought and Political Theory of Max Weber*, London, 1972.
26. *WL*, p. 605.

Bibliography
The Main Works of Max Weber

Gesammelte Aufsätze zur Religionssoziologie, 3 Vols., Tübingen, 1920/21.
Gesammelte Aufsätze zur Wissenschaftslehre, 3. erweiterte und verbesserte Auflage, ed. Johannes Winckelmann, Tübingen, 1968.
Gesammelte Politische Schriften, 3. erneut vermehrte Auflage, ed. Johannes Winckelmann, Tübingen, 1971.
Gesammelte Aufsätze zur Soziologie und Sozialpolitik, Tübingen, 1924.
Gesammelte Aufsätze zur Sozial- und Wirtschaftsgeschichte, Tübingen, 1924.
Wirtschaft und Gesellschaft. Grundriss der Verstehenden Soziologie, mit einem Anhang: Die rationalen und soziologischen Grundlagen der Musik, 4., neu herausgegebene Auflage, ed. Johannes Winckelmann, Tübingen, 1956.
Rechtssoziologie, aus dem Manuskript herausgegeben und eingeleitet von Johannes Winckelmann, 2. überarbeitete Auflage, 1967.
Wirtschaftsgeschichte, Abriß der Universalen Sozial- und Wirtschaftsgeschichte, ed. S. Hellmann and M. Palyi, 3rd Edition, München, 1958.

A. English Editions

From Max Weber: Essays in Sociology, trans. and ed. H. H. Gerth and C. Wright Mills, 6th impr., London, 1967.
Max Weber on the Methodology of the Social Sciences, ed. Edward A. Shils and Henry A. Finch, Glencoe, I., 1949.
The Protestant Ethic and the Spirit of Capitalism, trans. Talcott Parsons, London, 1965.
The Religion of China: Confucianism and Taoism, Glencoe, 1949.
The Religion of India: The Sociology of Hinduism and Buddism, Glencoe, 1958.
Ancient Judaism, Glencoe, 1952.
Economy and Society. An Outline of Interpretive Sociology, ed. Gunther Roth and Claus Wittich, New York, 1968 (with an important introduction).
General Economic History, trans. and ed. F. H. Knight, Glencoe, 1950.
The Sociology of Religion, Boston, 1967.

B. Secondary Literature

Abramowski Günther, *Das Geschichtsbild Max Webers. Universalgeschichte am Leitfaden des okzidentalen Rationalisierungsprozesses*, Stuttgart, 1966.

Andrewski, Stanislav, 'Method and Substantive Theory in Max Weber', *The British Journal of Sociology*, Vol. 15, 1964.

Antoni, Carlo, *From History to Sociology*, 1962.

Aron, Raymond, 'Max Weber und die Machtpolitik', *Zeitschrift f. Politik* 11, 1964 (also in *Max Weber und die Soziologie heute, Verhandlungen des 15. Deutschen Soziologentages*, ed. Stammer, Berlin, 1965).

――. *Main Currents in Sociological Thought*, Vol. 2, New York, 1967.

Ashcraft, Richard, 'Marx and Weber on Liberalism as Bourgeois Ideology', *Comparative Studies in Society and History*, Vol. 14, No. 2, 1972.

Baumgarten, Eduard, *Max Weber. Werk und Person*, Tübingen, 1964.

Bendix, Reinhard, *Max Weber. An Intellectual Portrait*, New York, 1960.

Bendix, Reinhard and Roth, Guenther, *Scholarship and Partisanship. Essays on Max Weber*, London, 1971.

Birnbaum, Norman, 'Conflicting Interpretations of the Rise of Capitalism', *The British Journal of Sociology*, Vol. 4, 1953.

Brunn, H. H., *Science Values and Politics in Max Weber's Methodology*, Copenhagen, 1972.

Cerny, 'Storm over Max Weber', *Encounter*, Vol. 23, 2, 1964.

Dronberger, Ilse, *The Political Thought of Max Weber. In Quest of Statesmanship.* New York, 1971.

Eisenstadt, S. N., *The Protestant Ethic and Modernization*, 1968.

Eldridge, J. T. (ed.), *Max Weber and the Interpretation of Social Reality*, London, 1972.

Falk, Werner, 'Democracy and Capitalism in Max Weber's, Sociology', *The Sociological Review*, Vol. 27, 1935.

Ferber, Christian von, *Die Gewalt in der Politik*, Stuttgart, 1970.

Fleischmann, E., 'De Weber à Nietzsche', *Archives Européennes de Sociologie*, Vol. 5., 1964.

Freund, Julien, *The Sociology of Max Weber*, New York, 1968.

Giddens, Anthony, *Capitalism and Modern Social Theory. An Analysis of the Writings of Marx, Durkheim and Max Weber*, Cambridge, 1971.

――. *Politics and Sociology in the Thought of Max Weber*, London, 1972.

Green, Robert W., *Protestantism and Capitalism. The Weber Thesis and its Critics*, New York, 1959.

Habermas, Jürgen, *Technik und Wissenschaft als Ideologie.* Surkamp, Neuwied, 1968.

Habermas, Jürgen and Luhmann, Nicklas, *Theorie der Gesellschaft oder Sozialtechnologie*, Surkamp, Neuwied, 1971.

Hattich, Manfred, 'Der Begriff des Politischen bei Max Weber', *Politische Vierteljahresschrift*, Vol. 8, 1967.

Henrich, Dieter, *Die Einheit der Wissenschaftslehre Max Webers*, Tübingen, 1952.

Reuss, Alfred, 'Max Weber und das Problem der Universalgeschichte', in: *Zur Theorie der Weltgeschichte*, Berlin, 1968.

――. 'Max Webers Bedeutung für die Geschichte des griechisch-römischen Altertums', *Historische Zeitschrift* Vol. 201, 1965.

Honigsheim, Paul, *On Max Weber, Collected Essays*, New York, 1968.

Hufnagel, Gerd, *Kritik als Beruf. Der kritische Gehalt im Werk Max Webers*, Frankfurt, 1971.

Hughes, Stuart H., *Consciousness and Society. The Re-Orientation of European Thought 1890–1930*. London, 1959.

Janoska-Bendl, Judith, *Methodologische Aspekte des Idealtypus. Max Weber und die Soziologie der Geschichte*, Berlin, 1965.

Jaspers, Karl, *Three Essays. Leonardo, Descartes, Max Weber.* Trans. Ralph Manheim, New York, 1964.

Kocka, Jürgen, 'Karl Marx und Max Weber. Ein methodologischer Vergleich', *Zeitschrift für die gesammte Staatswissenschaft*, Vol. 122, 1966.

Kolko, Gabriel, 'Max Weber on America: Theory and Evidence', *History and Theory*, Vol. 1, 1961.

Lachmann, Ludwig, M., *The Legacy of Max Weber: Three Essays*. London, 1970.

Lazarsfeld, P. and Oberschall, Antony, 'Max Weber and Empirical Social Research', *The American Sociological Review*, Vol. 30, 2, 1965.

Lefevre, Wolfgang, *Zum historischen Charakter und zur historischen Funktion der Methode bürgerlicher Soziologie. Untersuchung am Werk Webers.* Surkamp, Neuwied, 1972.

Lenk, Kurt, *Ideologie*. 2 ed., Neuwied, 1964.

Lindenlaub, Dieter, 'Richtungskämpfe im Verein für Sozialpolitik. Wissenschaft und Sozialpolitik im Kaiserreich, vornehmlich vom Beginn des "Neuen Kurses" bis zum Ausbruch des Ersten Weltkrieges 1890–1914', *Vierteljahresschrift für Sozial und Wirtschaftsgeschichte*, Beiheft 52/53, Wiesbaden, 1967.

Löwenstein, Karl, *Max Webers staatspolitische Auffassungen in der Sicht unserer Zeit*, Frankfurt, Bonn 1965-
———. English trans.: *Max Weber's Political Ideas in the Perspective of our Time*, 1966.

Löwith, Karl, 'Max Weber und Karl Marx' in: *Gesammelte Abhandlungen. Zur Kritik der geschichtlichen Existenz*, Stuttgart, 1969. (partially trans. in Dennis Wrong, *Makers of Modern Social Science, Max Weber*, Englewood Cliffs, N.Y., 1970.)
———. 'Max Weber und seine Nachfolger', *Mass und Wert*, Vol. 3, 1939–40.
———. 'Die Entzauberung der Welt durch Wissenschaft', *Merkur*, Vol. 18, 1964.

Luhmann, Nikolaus, 'Zweck – Herrschaft – System. Grundbegriffe und Prämissen Max Webers', *Der Staal*, Vol. 3, 1964.

Lukes, Steven, 'Methodological Individualism Reconsidered', *The British Journal of Sociology*, Vol. 19, 1968.

Lukács, Georg, *Die Zerstörung der Vernunft*, Berlin, 1955.

Lüthy, Herbert, 'Once Again: Calvinism and Capitalism', *Encounter*, Vol. 22, 1, 1964. (reprinted in Dennis Wrong, *Makers of Modern Social Science, Max Weber*, 1970.)

Marcuse, Herbert, 'Der Kampf gegen den Liberalismus in der totalitären Staatsauffassung' in: *Kultur und Gesellschaft I*, Surkamp, Neuwied, 1965. (first printed in *Zeitschrift für Sozialforschung*, Vol. 3, 2, Paris, 1934).
———. 'Industrialisierung und Kapitalismus' in: *Max Weber und die Soziologie heute. Verhandlungen des 15. Deutschen Soziologentages*, Tübingen, 1965.
English Version:
'Industrialisation and Capitalism', *New Left Review*, Vol. 30, 1965 (also in Stammer, *Max Weber and Sociology Today*, 1971.)

Mayer, Jacob Peter, *Max Weber and German Politics. A Study in Political Sociology*, 2nd ed. London, 1956.

McCormack, Th., 'The Protestant Ethic and the Spirit of Capitalism', *British Journal of Sociology*, Vol. 20, 1969.

Miller, S. M., *Max Weber.* New York, 1968.

Mitzman, Arthur, *The Iron Cage. An Historical Interpretation of Max Weber*, New York, 1970.

Mommsen, Wolfgang J., *Max Weber und die deutsche Politik, 1890–1920*, Tübingen, 1959.

———. 'Zurn Begriff der "plebiszitaren Führerdemokratie" bei Max Weber', *Kölner Zeitschrift für Soziologie und Sozialpsychologie*, Vol. 15, 1963.

———. 'Max Weber's Political Sociology and his Philosophy of World History', *International Social Science Journal*, Vol. 17, 1965. (some extracts from this are published in: Dennis Wrong, *Makers of Modern Political Science, Max Weber*, New York, 1970.)

———. 'Universalgeschichtliches und politisches Denken bei Max Weber", *Historische Zeitschrift* Vol. 201, 1965.

———. 'Die Vereinigten Staaten von Amerika im politischen Denken Max Webers', *Historische Zeitschrift*, Vol. 213, 1971.

———. 'Max Weber', in: *Deutsche Historiker, III* ed. H.-U. Wehler, pp. 65–90, Göttingen, 1972.

Nisbet, Robert A., *The Sociological Tradition*, New York, 1966.

Nolte, Ernst, 'Max Weber vor dem Faschismus', *Der Staat*, Vol. 2, 1963.

Oberschall, Anthony, *Empirical Social Research in Germany, 1848–1914*, The Hague, 1965.

Parsons, Talcott, *The Structure of Social Action*, Vol. II, 2 ed., reprinted, New York, 1968.

———. *Essays in Sociological Theory*, revised ed., Glencoe, Ill., 1954.

Rex, John, *Key Problems of Sociological Theory*, London, 1961.

———. 'Max Weber', in: Timothy Raison, ed., *The Founding Fathers of Social Science*, Harmondsworth, 1969.

———. 'Typology and Objectivity: a Comment on Weber's four Sociological Methods', in: Arun Sahay, *Max Weber and Modern Sociology*, London, 1971.

Ringer, Fritz, K., *The Decline of the German Mandarins: The German Academic Community 1890–1933*, Cambridge, 1969.

Robertson, H. M., *Aspects of the Rise of Economic Individualism. A Criticism of Max Weber and his School*, Cambridge, 1933.

Rogers, Rolf E., *Max Weber's Ideal Type Theory*, New York, 1969.

Runciman, W. G., *Social Science and Political Theory*, Cambridge, 1965.

———. *A Critique of Max Weber's Philosophy of Social Science*, Cambridge U. P., 1972.

Sahey, Arun (ed.), *Max Weber and Modern Sociology*, London, 1971.

Samuelson, Kurt, *Religion and Economic Action*, ed. D. C. Coleman, Stockholm, 1961.

Schelting, Alexander von, *Max Weber's Wissenschaftslehre. Das logische Problem der Kulturerkenntnis*, Tübingen, 1934.

Schluchter, Wolfgang, *Wertfreiheit und Verantwortungsethik. Zum Verhältnis von Wissenschaft und Politik bei Max Weber*, Tübingen, 1971.

Schmidt, Gustav, *Deutscher Historismus und der Übergang zur parlamentarischen Demokratie. Untersuchungen zu den politischen Gedanken von Meinecke, Troeltsch, Max Weber*, Hamburg, 1964.

Schulz, Gerhard, 'Geschichtliche Theorie und politisches Denken bei Max Weber', *Vierteljahreshefte für Zeitgeschichte*, Vol. 12, 1964.

Simey, T. S., 'Max Weber: Man of Affairs or Theoretical Sociologist?', *Sociological Review*, Vol. 14, 1966.

———. 'Weber's Sociological Theory of Value: An Appraisal in Mid-Century', *The Sociological Review*, Vol. 13, 1965.

Spencer, Martin E., 'Weber on Legitimate Norms and Authority', *British Journal of Sociology*, Vol. 21, 1970.

Stammer, Otto (ed.), *Max Weber und die Soziologie Heute. Verhandlungen des 15. Deutschen Soziologentages*, Tübingen, 1965. English edition: *Max Weber and Sociology Today*, Oxford, Blackwell, 1971.

Streisand, Joachim, 'Max Weber: Soziologie, Politik und Geschichtsschreibung', *Studien über die deutsche Geschichtswissenschaft*, Vol. 2, ed. J. Streisand, Berlin, 1965.

Tawney, Richard H., *Religion and the Rise of Capitalism*, Harmondsworth, 1964.

Tenbruck, Friedrich H., 'Die Genesis der Methodologie Max Webers', *Kölner Zeitschrift für Soziologie und Sozialpsychologie*, Vol. 11, 1959.

Topitsch, Ernst, 'Max Webers Geschichtsauffassung', *Wissenschaft und Weltbild*, Vol. 3, 1950.

Weber, Marianne, *Max Weber. Ein Lebensbild*. Tübingen, 1926; Neudruck, Heidelberg, 1950.

'Max Weber zum Gedächtnis', ed. René König and Johannes Winckelmann, Sonderheft 7 der *Kölner Zeitschrift für Soziologie und Sozialpsychologie*, Köln Opladen, 1963.

Wegener, Walther, *Die Quellen der Wissenschaftsauffassung Max Webers und die Problematik der Werturteilsfreiheit in der Nationalokonomie. Ein wissens soziologischer Beitrag*, Berlin, 1962.

Weyembergh, Maurice, *Le Voluntarisme rationnel de Max Weber*, Brussels, I 97 r.

Winckelmann, Johannes, *Gesellschaft und Staat in der verstehenden Soziologie Max Webers*, Tübingen, 1957.

———. 'Max Webers "opus Posthumum"', *Zeitschrift für die gesammte Staatswissenschaft*, Vol. 105, 1948–49.

Wrong, Dennis (ed.), *Makers of Modern Social Science: Max Weber*, Englewood Cliffs, New Jersey, 1970.

Postscript

Volker R. Berghahn

Although Wolfgang Mommsen's book also examined other aspects of Weber's thought, he considered his writings on the socio-economic and cultural impact of industrial capitalism to be a key to our understanding of the modern world. This Postscript represents an attempt to trace the evolution of capitalism and bureaucracy during the century since Weber's death in 1920. Up to that date, he had continued to write about capitalism and bureaucracy within a framework that Wolfgang Mommsen examined so concisely in the five chapters of this book. Weber had focused on the growth of those two phenomena before 1914 and had looked not only at the concentration of economic power in ever bigger share-holding corporations but also at how the public and private sectors continued to undergo a process of bureaucratization. Jürgen Kocka was among the first historians to trace this latter process with respect to the electrical engineering firm of Siemens. He showed in his book that, instead of being driven by dynamic and restless managers constantly rooting for change, Siemens's salaried employees developed a civil service mentality.[1] Their loyalty to the firm was more important than fast upward mobility. They accepted also the principle of seniority, calculated by years of service rather than preferential promotion of promising and ambitious younger 'high-flyers'.

While Weber had observed these changes in capitalism and bureaucracy before the First World War, he had also been preoccupied with many other topics, such as the role of religion and faith-based associations. What for many years undermined his energy was that he suffered from poor health and mental problems and had to take longer leaves from his teaching. Once the War had broken out, he became involved in the heated domestic debates on Germany's war aims and impact of nationalism more generally. With Weber's passing at age 56, it was left to scholarship of the post-war decades to take up the study of the changes that both capitalism and bureaucracy underwent after the war had become ever more total.[2] The growing mobilization of all material and mental resources in the name of achieving ultimate victory inevitably led to a centralization not only of government but also of the organization of the capitalist economies by the employers and their interest groups, with the trade unions appearing as a third factor.

It seems that this ever more thorough war-time organization of society inspired the Marxist theoretician Rudolf Hilferding to conceptualize what he was observing. In this respect he was able to build on an influential book that he had written about the structural evolution of capitalism before the outbreak of war in his book *Finanzkapital*, translated into English many years later as *Finance Capital. A Study of the Latest Phase of Capitalist Development*.[3] As the war dragged on, Hilferding came to believe that what he saw was in fact a new phase in the bureaucratization and concentration of capitalist production. While Weber probably knew about *Finanzkapital* and as a critic of Marxism disapproved of it, he began to ponder the impact of the war in terms of the conditions of a 'successful peace'.[4] This peace envisioned, apart from social reforms, a far-reaching recasting of the Reich constitution with regard to Prussia and citizenship. However, the deteriorating situation of the Hohenzollern monarchy, its defeat in 1918 and the subsequent revolutionary upheavals made the systematic pursuit of his ideas increasingly difficult. With his health also progressively declining, Weber died in June 1920, a few weeks after right-wing radicals unsuccessfully tried to overthrow the parliamentary-democratic Weimar Republic.

While Weber's voluminous writings continued to occupy subsequent generations of sociologists and historians in a great variety of ways, his passing provides a good point at which to move more specifically to a discussion of the 'Age of Capitalism and Bureaucracy' beyond the life of the famous sociologist. The aim is to examine how this Age unfolded in historical reality and how scholars, politicians and entrepreneurs dealt with its challenges during the rest of the twentieth century and the beginning of the twenty-first. Weber lived long enough to witness the outbreak and course of the revolution in Russia and the seizure of power by the Bolsheviks under the leadership of Vladimir Lenin in the autumn of 1917. Thenceforth the world not only became divided into two camps economically, politically and ideologically, but in its eastern half also came to be dominated by a regime that, in order to secure and consolidate its position, deployed the bureaucratic infrastructures of the former Tsarist state and of the newly founded Red Army to rebuild a high level of wartime centralization.[5] Lenin proclaimed that his regime was governed by 'democratic centralism', but in fact his rule was profoundly undemocratic and dictatorial. It has been argued that he had no choice but to establish this regime if he wanted to win the civil war that both the Russian counter-revolutionaries and the Western Allies had launched to nip Bolshevism in the bud. Lenin's rule was accompanied by the expropriation not only of the commercial and industrial capitalists who had emerged in Tsarist Russia, but also of the land-owners who took up arms against him.

However, the Bolshevik regime was not merely a product of an emergency under which Lenin felt he was forced to rally his forces; autocratic rule was also inherent in Bolshevik ideology and strategy after Lenin and his associates had transformed their movement into a cadre party that would not wait until the proletariat was ready to stage a revolution from below, as Rosa Luxemburg, Lenin's great counterpart among radical Marxists before 1914, had insisted. And so Lenin used his disciplined Bolshevik cadres to seize power by unleashing a violent revolution from above. It was thus both Lenin's political determination and Leninist ideology that set Russia, soon to be called Soviet Union, on a path of centralized bureaucratic rule and economic management. There was the brief period of the New Economic Policy in 1922 when the regime encouraged entrepreneurial initiative, especially in agriculture; but this phase came to an end after Lenin's death in 1924 and the victory of Joseph Stalin in his subsequent power struggle with Leon Trotsky, Nicolai Bukharin, Lev Kamenev and Alexander Zinoviev.[6] A very shrewd bureaucrat himself, he set the Soviet Union on a path of forced industrialization from above at the cost of millions of lives among the well-to-do farmers (kulaks) and countless other opponents of his regime during the Great Purges of the 1930s.

Meanwhile the West had emerged from the ordeal of World War I facing different pressures and with a different agenda. The Allied engagement in the Russian civil war was designed to destroy the Leninist socio-economic model and to rescue not merely Europe's traditional governmental bureaucracies but also capitalism from the enormous human and material devastation that the total war of 1914–1918 had left behind in Europe. The only country that had come out of this conflict strengthened was the United States both in terms of its financial and industrial power and its international prestige.[7] There were two strong currents across the Atlantic that pushed America to use its newly found clout. To begin with, the national economy and its industries had to be reconverted to the production of civilian goods. But given the considerable productive capacities and also the financial resources that American banks had accumulated, it was clear that the pent-up demand for civilian goods back home might not be sufficient to sustain postwar domestic stabilization and prosperity. As a result, the big corporations were also looking for an expansion of their business to foreign markets, and to Europe, the most important prewar market, in particular.

Thus it did not take long before American businessmen travelled to Europe to gain a first-hand impression of the situation and the potential for reconstruction. What they witnessed were millions of widowed women and orphaned children, and large numbers of veterans returning from the front, all of them starving. Together with the male and female blue-collar workers who had been producing arms, these veterans constituted a formidable workforce ready to resume production, if only investments were made in their factories to replace clapped-out machinery. This is where Frank Vanderlip, the former president of the National City Bank (NCB), came in.[8] Having seen the poverty and devastation on his trip to Europe, this Wall Street banker developed a plan for floating a huge private loan, also with contributions from Swedish and Swiss banks, to revive the European economies and to create export opportunities for both American goods as well as loans. This plan might have done the trick of pulling American and European capitalism out of its deep hole. The money required for these reconstruction loans was in principle available. But capitalists, and bankers in particular, tend to be cautious people. Fearing that Vanderlip's plan might fail, they turned to Washington's politicians asking them to underwrite its costs. Should the initiative hit the rocks, it was not the private banks that would have been liable, but the public purse and hence ultimately the ordinary American taxpayers. The trouble was that the American public was not willing to secure those reconstruction loans. Americans had been reluctant to enter the war before April 1917 and, while the American contribution to the Allied victory was crucial when troops finally arrived in France in the spring of 1918, once the guns had fallen silent, they wanted the Army to 'send the boys home' without delay and retreat to the North American continent, leaving the Europeans to sort out their problems.

This mood was part of a wide-spread reluctance to follow the political ideas of U.S. President Woodrow Wilson.[9] He envisioned not only a revival of the type of liberal capitalism that had existed before 1914, but also a new international political order that would abandon traditional diplomacy and develop a new type of bureaucracy that would administer a Wilsonian international system based on the principles of equality among its members and peaceful cooperation, facilitated by a newly created League of Nations. The administrators who were to run this organization were appointed to be servants of a new internationalism committed to the preservation of peace and conflict resolution. It was therefore a serious blow when the United States refused to join this effort. Although the Covenant of the League contained articles and instruments of enforcement, it lacked public political support and thus remained weak from the start. And with the rise of fascism in Europe and of Japanese militarism in the 1930s it was subsequently pushed aside by a violent nationalism with its brutal expansionist ambitions. These weaknesses became visible as early as 1919 at the time of the peace conference in Paris at which Wilson's ideas of establishing a new international order were defeated and the pre-1914 principles of traditional power diplomacy reasserted themselves. Wilson left Europe disillusioned, and peace was imposed on the defeated countries by Europe's nationalist politicians and their reliance on the expertise of their own traditional ministerial bureaucracies.[10] This continuity of personnel applied not merely to the pursuit of national-interest politics but also to domestic administration. Instead of pacific reconciliation between former enemies there was confrontation, especially over the thorny question of Allied reparations to be paid by the vanquished. The age of bureaucracy with the rise of the expert that Weber had been worrying about in his lifetime thus remained a key factor in the evolution of the state after 1918.

By 1923 the tensions that these postwar conflicts had generated had escalated to the point where France and Belgium decided to occupy the Ruhr region, the industrial heartland of Germany, to collect reparations in kind. The German population responded with passive resistance, resulting in the collapse of the economy and an attempt by Adolf Hitler and Erich Ludendorff to seize political power in Berlin in November 1923.[11] As France was also forced to devalue its currency, European politics took a disastrous turn, but it also gave American bankers an opportunity to find a way out of the crisis, this time without guarantees by the American taxpayer. In 1924, they negotiated the Dawes Plan that provided for a carefully calibrated programme of regular and staggered reparations payments by Germany which in turn cleared the way not only for American direct investments, but also for loans.[12] The optimism behind the floating of these funds through the major American banks was buttressed by a boom in the U.S. economy during the mid-1920s that was stimulated by the breakthrough of what had come to be known as 'Fordism'.[13] Already before 1914, Henry Ford and other entrepreneurs had developed the idea not only of rationalizing the production of automobiles by introducing assembly-line work. They had also decided not to pocket all the gains of greater profitability for themselves and their shareholders, but to pass some of them on to the buyers of their cars by reducing prices. These reductions were tangible enough to make it possible for consumers who before 1914 could not have afforded a car, to buy one by the mid-twenties, often with the help of hire-purchase agreements with banks that advanced the funds for the purchase.

However, it was not just automobiles that became affordable to the average American consumer in this way, but also other consumer durables, such as stoves and washing machines. This development was facilitated by the impact of the Sherman and Clayton Acts of 1890 and 1912.[14] These pieces of Congressional legislation banned the formation of monopolies and cartels, i.e., horizontal agreements between independent firms to regulate their production and prices and pursue other restrictive practices. In other words, Sherman was designed to secure the principle of capitalist competition among companies within the same branch. Thus a welter of other manufacturers now marketed their cars next to Ford's who would observe the pricing practices of his competitors very carefully. If Sherman prohibited the building of monopolies, it did not stop the merger of companies and hence the growth of ever more powerful corporations. American capitalism became oligopolistic, securing competition in the marketplace and facilitating the consumer boom of the mid-1920s. In the late 1920s, the United States experienced a more widespread prosperity, enjoyed by mostly white middle-class Americans, while African-Americans were once more left behind. Stocks saw a phenomenal rise, with most gains made by the big corporations of the consumer and entertainment sectors. Believing that a growing investment portfolio and generous dividend payments would make them rich, many Americans who had savings in the bank began to speculate. They took great risks in the expectation that the boom would last forever. As John K. Galbraith put it in his study of the depression that followed, it was not 'the massiveness of participation' in this quest for wealth that was so striking; 'rather it was the way [this speculation] became central to [American] culture'.[15]

What these gamblers forgot was that modern capitalism was also prone to recessions and even depressions, and this is what hit United States from October 1929, triggering the Great Slump of the 1930s.[16] This catastrophe that bankrupted countless businesses, large and small, and led to mass unemployment in Europe and the United States was exacerbated by the fact that many wartime restrictions of the economy had been rescinded. American capitalism in particular had returned to the largely unregulated economic liberalism of the pre-1914 period. As the crisis spread, the first response by governments and their bureaucracies was to cut public expenditures and to adopt an austerity programme that made the predicament of the unemployed and their families only worse. There was an alternative solution that is most prominently associated with the name of the British economist John Maynard Keynes: He insisted that a depression required not a cutting of public expenditure; instead public funds should be pumped into the stagnant economy, even at the cost of increasing government deficits.[17] This injection would enable firms, anxious to restart production, to hire workers who, with wages once more in their pockets, would in turn spend it on consumer goods. They would also begin to pay taxes and social security contributions that would shrink the deficit. The earlier increase in the public debt would start to decline and the economy would begin to grow again.

The experience of the United States in these years of a severe crisis of capitalism is a good case in point for testing these theories. President Herbert Hoover had still adhered to an orthodox austerity programme that kept cutting public expenditures. His successor Franklin D. Roosevelt developed, when assuming the presidency in 1933, a programme of Keynesian deficit spending and investments in public works, such as that of the Tennessee Valley Authority (TVA) and other big building projects.[18] Being very experimental, Roosevelt's New Deal to uplift a depressed economy and to salvage capitalism inevitably experienced a string of setbacks whose significance has preoccupied several generations of economic historians. Still, overall it was a success and was also popular with the voters, the more so as it was accompanied by the implementation of social insurance programmes that protected workers. They could also form trade unions, protected by law, to represent their interests. Roosevelt's New Deal has been criticized by some who asserted that it was only the boost of military production once the United States had joined the war in 1941 that overcame the Great Depression.[19] What this interpretation tends to downplay was the prewar effect of Roosevelt's decision to lay the foundations for this later boost between 1937 and 1940 by covertly placing orders for military hardware. Supported by Treasury Secretary Henry Morgenthau, who was even more concerned about the rise of Nazi Germany, Fascist Italy and expansionist Japan than the President, the White House now adopted what might be called a 'military Keynesianism' that required an enhanced participation of the Federal bureaucracy.

However, Roosevelt's Keynesianism had from 1933 had a competitor in Germany when Hitler, also concerned with getting industrial production going and reducing Germany's massive unemployment, invested public monies in heavy industry to produce coal, steel, but also military equipment.[20] Hitler's armament orders, though, were placed with another goal in mind: They were not meant to stimulate a civilian economy and civilian consumption, but to be deployed in a future war with the aim of conquering 'living space' and ruthlessly exploiting the human and material resources of the defeated nations of Europe and the Soviet Union. While we should be careful to push the parallels between the two countries too far, one point must nevertheless be made in terms of the evolution of post-Weberian capitalism and bureaucracy: Unlike in the nineteenth century, when liberal capitalism insisted that the state must keep out of the economy and that it was for the 'market' to provide the guidelines for entrepreneurial decisionmaking, in the 1930s bureaucrats and capitalists, traumatized by the Great Depression, had moved more closely together to form a cooperative relationship. The task was for the two sides to manage the national economy, with the trade unions potentially being a third factor of corporate cooperation. In the United States these unions were still too weak to gain a position of equality, whereas in Germany, Italy and Japan they were either brutally repressed or relegated to a very marginal role.[21]

If one compares these developments of capitalism and state power in the 1930s with Weber's thoughts as presented by Mommsen in his volume, it is not difficult to see why the former would have been quite unhappy, had he still lived to see Germany's development in the years before World War II. As indicated in Mommsen's chapter entitled 'A Liberal in Despair', he tended to be quite pessimistic about the future of modern industrial societies, believing that its inhabitants would increasingly be dominated by the expert not only in the public sphere, but also in the private-capitalist economy.[22] Both of them would ultimately put the individual into an 'iron cage of serfdom'. While these were Weber's pre-1920 conjectures, with the benefit of hindsight we are now on firmer ground and can turn to some of the interpreters of capitalism and bureaucracy in the 1930s who actually lived to witness the evolution of the two. One of the most influential social scientists who tried to conceptualize this age was James Burnham. He is an interesting theoretician because of his own ideological journey from Trotskyism to his study of the *Managerial Revolution*, which he claimed in 1941 was an account of *What Is Happening in the World*.[23] To begin with, in toying with Trotsky's concept of 'permanent revolution' up to the achievement of the much vaunted socialist society, he not only showed that he knew his Marxism-Leninism, but that he was also opposed to Stalin's bureaucratic path of forced industrialization, all the more so after Trotsky had been forced to flee to Mexico where Stalin's henchmen eventually assassinated him in 1940.[24]

Given his ideological past, Burnham was also convinced that liberal capitalism had failed. It was to be replaced by a different system, elements of which he saw in the Soviet Union, Hitler's Nazi regime as well as in Roosevelt's New Deal. All three types of socio-economic and political order, he postulated, were dominated by a class of managers who were driven not only by a quest for economic privilege, but also by an ambition to gain *Herrschaft* in both the corporate and the political spheres. And yet, Burnham was careful not to put all industrial societies in the same box. For him there were still important differences between systems in which an elite of managers was operating within a statist framework and supported by an infrastructure of party functionaries acting as typical Weberian bureaucrats, like in the Soviet Union, on the one hand, and, on the other, a system based on private ownership and owner-appointed corporate managers cooperating with a still democratic political framework.

To Burnham, there was yet another difference between American New Deal capitalism and its administrative infrastructure, on the one hand, and the peculiar type of capitalism that had emerged in Germany. It had diverged from the competitive, though oligopolistic capitalism of the post-Sherman United States, when Germany took the turn toward cartels and monopolies.[25] Legitimated by a decision of the Reich Court, horizontal agreements between independent firms were thenceforth legally protected arrangements of commercial cooperation. After a late nineteenth-century start, this system proliferated in Imperial Germany and even more so in the post-1918 Weimar Republic, creating a very peculiar capitalism in which competition had been replaced by collusion and had resulted in powerful cartels and syndicates (sales cartels that looked after a coordinated marketing of the products of a particular branch of industry).

This development was complemented in the 1920s by the emergence of virtual monopolies in at least two branches. The most typical was the IG Farben conglomerate that dominated the domestic market, while competing overseas with foreign corporations, such as Du Pont in the US and Britain's Imperial Chemical Industries (ICI). The other example is Vereinigte Stahlwerke, founded in 1926 as a cooperative agreement of key companies in the German coal and steel industries that also became a virtual monopoly.[26] To be sure, these conglomerates were still privately owned corporations, buttressed by their own bureaucracies. But their significance also came to lie in the fact that after 1933 the Hitler dictatorship preferred to cooperate with these cartels and monopolies that simplified the Nazis' quest of centralizing the economy in preparation of a future war of conquest and exploitation.

This German capitalist system (and the similarly organized Japanese *zaibatsu* system) clashed in World War II with an American capitalism constrained by the Sherman and Clayton Acts. If Hitler had won his war against Stalin in the East in 1941, as he confidently expected to, there is little doubt that he would not only have organized the conquered space along the lines of his racist ideology, but would have taken this Germanic bloc out of the international economy. His aim was to achieve autarky, not a return to multilateral trade among nations. No less important, this bloc would have been organized as a 'Closed Space Cartel' (Grossraumkartell), as the economist Arno Sölter entitled his blueprint book of 1941 when German industrialists, the functionaries of the Reich Economics Ministry and other government agencies began to ransack the occupied territories and to reorganize European markets along cartel lines.[27]

It is not difficult to see that this re-ordering of Europe along economic and racist lines was anathema to Roosevelt and his advisors when they began to realize the seriousness of the threat posed by the three Axis powers. Politically, Washington represented, and had sworn, to defend a democratic Constitution based a division of powers and parliamentary representation. However, the war against Germany was not just about the future organization of the American political system. It was also about the principles of how to run a modern capitalist-industrial economy. This was put very clearly by no lesser person than Roosevelt himself when towards the end of the war he defined America's economic war aims as follows: 'During the past have century, the United States has developed a tradition of opposition to private monopolies. The Sherman and Clayton Acts have become as much part of the American way of life as the Due Process clause of the Constitution. By protecting the consumer against monopoly these statutes guarantee him the benefits of competition . . . Unfortunately, a number of foreign countries, particularly in continental Europe, do not possess such a tradition against cartels. On the contrary, cartels have received encouragement from these governments. Especially this is true with respect to Germany. Moreover, cartels were utilized by the Nazis as governmental instrumentalities to achieve political ends. . . . Defeat of the Nazi armies will have to be followed by the eradication of these weapons of economic warfare. But more than the elimination of the political activities of German cartels will be required. Cartel practices which restrict the free flow of goods in foreign commerce will have to be curbed'.[28] He might have added that they would also have to be replaced by something similar, though not identical, to the American system of democratic politics and a competitive, if oligopolistic capitalism geared towards an Open Door multilateral world trading system without autarkic blocs.

However, in the conception of the American political and economic elites a defeat of Hitler did not mean a return to a pre-1914 liberal capitalism. Although there was a push-back by parts of the business community against extending Roosevelt's New Deal into the postwar period, the cooperative relationship between industry, the trade unions and the Federal government proved stronger and continued. Reconversion to civilian production was achieved more quickly this time than after 1918. Consequently, the United States was able to take off in the 1950s into the type of Fordist consumer capitalism, the rise of which the country had first seen in the mid-1920s. Its success was also driven by the onset in 1946/47 of the Cold War between the Soviet Bloc and the Western Allies. With the authoritarian and fascist solutions to organizing a modern industrial society having been defeated, the ideological and power-political differences that the wartime alliance between Stalin, Roosevelt and Churchill had covered up due to the necessity of defeating Germany, Italy and Japan, resurfaced in 1947/48. Rejecting Stalinist political autocracy and Moscow's centralized economic planning, the American ways of managing both economic and political problems through cooperation between business, trade unions and government seemed to offer a better constitutional framework for building a prosperous future for all citizens than the communist model.

If the struggle against fascism had stressed the threat of domination by Hitler's bureaucrats in cooperation with a highly cartelized German capitalism, the spectre of a Stalinist bureaucracy of the 1930s was still lurking in the background. The Allied effort to defeat fascism had put the earlier American rejection of the Soviet model on the backburner. Once victory had been achieved, the former systemic differences resurfaced. Now the fight was no longer against fascist totalitarianism, but against the centralist Stalinist ways of organizing an industrial society. By 1946/47, East-West tensions had become a 'Cold War'. But its onset had one further benefit in that it brought the United States and Western Europe together. This in turn facilitated Washington's decision not to repeat the mistake of 1919/20. Instead of refusing public funds to underwrite Vanderlip's reconstruction loan plan, as Congress had done after World War I, they promulgated the European Recovery Program in 1947/48.[29] Announced by secretary of state George C. Marshall in June 1947, this time it was the politicians who took the lead. By using taxpayers' monies they signalled to American private enterprise that it was safe to invest in European and even West German companies and to turn them into engines of reconstruction. A new era of capitalist growth began.

No less important, the new prosperity of the 1950s was accompanied by a further expansion of the welfare state, just as the Keynesian public investments programmes continued in the United States, especially through the construction of a highway system that complemented the long-distance railroad network and the modernization of urban commuter transit. While the Republican Party under U.S. president Dwight D. Eisenhower embodied this trilateral managerial welfare capitalism, it received a fresh impetus in 1961 when the Democrats came to power and John F. Kennedy, with vice president Lyndon Johnson at his side, embarked upon a programme of further social reform and the promotion of civil rights for discriminated minorities. No less important, the assassination of Kennedy in 1963 did not put a stop to these plans. With Johnson as Kennedy's successor, his idea was to lay the foundations of a 'Great Society' that included the introduction of universal healthcare for all. It envisaged the building of a more just and egalitarian society that integrated the African-American minority and other marginalized groups that had raised their voice in the civil rights movement.[30]

Although racist prejudice against the black and brown populations was deeply ingrained, there was plenty of optimism inside the big corporations, among American blue-collar workers and also among reform-minded politicians and social scientists that Johnson's strategy would work. Interestingly enough, the early 1960s were also the moment when the role of technocracy was being discussed again in the social sciences and trade unions whose leaders and members were concerned about its impact on the future of manufacturing and labour.[31] By the later 1960s, Johnson's optimism was beginning to fade and his vision of a 'Great Society' had to be abandoned when it could not be funded in the face of the rising costs of Washington's war in Southeast Asia. However, before exploring this chapter of American welfare capitalism and the role of its bureaucracies in it, the story of evolution of the New Deal economy of the 1950s must be complemented by an analysis of the economies of Europe during the Cold War. Overall, this region also came under the spell of the Open Door capitalist trading system spearheaded by the United States after 1945 during its confrontation with the Soviet Bloc. With Washington's encouragement, the European Coal and Steel Community (ECSC) had been created in 1951 as a new type of integrated trading bloc that, unlike the British Empire and Commonwealth, was not, however, designed as a customs union with preferential tariffs.[32] Some of its protagonists, such as Jean Monnet, even saw the ECSC as a first step to the creation of an open market covering all goods and the eventual creation of something like the United States of Europe.

While, like the American New Dealers, these Europeans promoted a welfare capitalism with strong trade unions and a management of the national economy in a trilateral arrangement between the two sides of industry and the state, its roots were different. Some of these roots went back to the early twentieth century and the introduction and expansion of a still embryonic social security net that provided unemployment benefits and insurance schemes for retirement and against illness, especially in Germany and Britain. The devastating impact of World War I resulted in an expansion of these programmes until most of them were virtually wiped out by the Great Depression of the 1930s. What followed was an even more destructive world war that again left millions of Europeans destitute and starving. With British Labour gaining power in London in August 1945, prime minister Clement Attlee was not the only politician wedded to the introduction of a National Health Service for all and a strengthening of social security.[33] But he was also determined radically to transform British capitalism, beginning with the nationalization of the coal and steel industries. Similar pressures to expropriate and put private industries and banks into the hands of politicians and civil servants existed in other West European countries as well as in the Western zones of occupation in defeated Germany. However, the search for a third way between American capitalism and Soviet communism soon faltered. It was again the Cold War that put a stop to these efforts, and the perceived threat of falling under Stalinist rule moved the societies of Western and Southern Europe back into the camp of a reformist capitalism, aided also by the American funding of European reconstruction and concomitant political pressures by Washington.

It is against this background that all Western European nations restored and strengthened their tattered welfare systems. The Western zones of occupation of Germany (that became the semi-sovereign Federal Republic of Germany in 1949) are a particularly good example of this need to build a strong social security system on the foundations of the Weimar German welfare state. The millions of refugees from now Soviet-occupied Eastern Europe, the war widows and orphans, the returning veterans and bombed-out families, the former foreign slave workers in Nazi industries and survivors of the concentration and extermination camps could not be left to their own devices and exposed to the harsh winds of an unrestrained capitalism. While, by the mid-1950s, a new postwar American consumer society began to spill over into Western Europe, there emerged, in parallel with the New Deal welfare state across the Atlantic, an infrastructure of a reformist West German capitalism that came to be called 'Social Market Economy'.[34] There was also the 1951 law of parity co-determination that gave employers, workers, and trade unions equal representation on the supervisory boards of the coal and steel companies as well as a 'worker director' with equal rights on the management board.[35]

If this was the shape of a postwar capitalism that unfolded in the West in the 1950s and, from the mid-1960s, was also expected to give birth to a Johnsonian 'Great Society' in the United States, it was the war in Southeast Asia and its escalating costs that sank not only Johnson's presidency, replacing it with Richard Nixon's Watergate Republicanism, but also with a neo-liberal capitalism. Its ideological precepts were first tried out under the presidency of Jimmy Carter.[36] After the trilateral management of the economy just could not lift the United States out of its post-Vietnam 'stagflation', that was exacerbated by the collapse of the Bretton Woods currency agreement and the first oil price shock of 1974, the extended crisis enabled the resurgence of radical left-wing debates about the future of 'late capitalism' and its replacement by a reformist socialism in which the state would again have an expanded role of societal management. It is in this context that some historians and social scientists began to develop the notion of 'Organized Capitalism' that they traced back to World War I.[37] However, their arguments about the links between capitalism and bureaucracy remained largely confined to the German case and merely stimulated a debate on whether it was applicable to other Western economies.

At the same time there emerged neo-liberal interpretations of the political economies of the West, and they now experienced a truly remarkable rise. Its promoters had been waiting in the wings since 1945, but were persistently sidelined by the advocates of a Keynesian management of the economy. Their alternative recipe was to eject governments and trade unions from their central role in the national economy and to stop leaving things to the working-out of trilateral compromises to secure steady growth, low unemployment and international exchange. Instead, it was to be left to the forces of 'The Market' to restore the dynamic expansion of production and prosperity.

The implications of this vision of a capitalist economy were very openly articulated by Milton Friedman and other theoreticians of neo-liberalism who postulated that the only social responsibility of the capitalist manager was to secure the profitability of his enterprise.[38] This meant that the influence of the state had to be pushed back; public expenditures had to be cut to facilitate tax reductions favouring the wealthy. This would encourage them to invest after a reduction of bureaucratic regulation and the influence of civil servants. Apart from government bureaucracies, the influence of trade unions that were also viewed as highly bureaucratized, was likewise to be curbed. The economist Arthur Laffer argued that these new policies would encourage investors to invest in the modernization of industries and that their dynamism would in turn have a 'trickle down' effect, resulting in the growth of the incomes of ordinary families. When it came to the question of where these investments would go, there was the traditional role of banks to support national, regional and local manufacturing. However, in the meantime the Open Door and internationalization of the markets had given an enormous boost to investment banks, many of them based in the City of London and the New York's Wall Street. They operated globally and their wealthy clients from around the world expected them to find markets that promised the highest returns.

By the 1980s, these neo-liberal ideas were no longer alluring theoretical constructs for academic debate. Two powerful politicians, looking for ways out of 'stagflation', were particularly attracted by the promises of governmental retreat, trade union diminution, and 'trickle-down': British prime minister Margaret Thatcher and U.S. president Ronald Reagan.[39] Coming to power with a clear parliamentary majority in 1979, Thatcher set the pace, with Reagan following in 1981, although he was more hamstrung in the implementation of his economic policies by American Federalism. Having restructured labour relations, cut taxes as well as public expenditures, and having begun the transformation of capitalism from a socially responsible stakeholder society to a shareholder society à la Friedman, Thatcher took the final step in 1987 by triggering the 'Big Bang'. It liberated the British banking system, concentrated in the London City, from its bureaucratic regulations that had constrained it from becoming the financial hub of global investment. What now took place was the 'financialization' of British capitalism and the domination of the banks to the detriment of British manufacturing. The longterm de-industrialization of the British economy that had begun before 1914 reached a new phase, with the old industrial regions of the English North now becoming wastelands, while the southern counties around London experienced great prosperity, based not on the production of goods, but on the global circulation of private wealth.

Meanwhile Reagan's neo-liberalism had been following British Thatcherism more slowly along a similar path. It was in the 1990s that U.S. president Bill Clinton, under the influence of neo-liberals such as Robert Rubin in his cabinet, and Alan Greenspan as chairman of the Federal Reserve Bank in Washington, scrapped Roosevelt's Glass-Steagall Act of 1933 that had put a firewall between the domestic banks as lenders to local industry, on the one hand, and huge investment banks, such as Goldman Sachs, on the other. The latter were free to tap into both the resources of wealthy clients from overseas and traditional American savings banks, now also lured by the opportunities of the global market.[40] Among the players of this market were, next the fantastically rich Arab oil families, also the Russian oligarchs who, after the collapse of the Soviet Bloc in 1990/91 had, in kleptocratic fashion, acquired the best pieces of the Russian economic pie. Especially its erstwhile nationalized corporations, run by bureaucrats, now fell into the hands of private entrepreneurs, attracted not only by the profitable ownership of huge conglomerates, but also by the ideas of Western neo-liberalism. What was left of the failed Soviet bureaucratic experiment were the former inequalities between elites and ordinary Russians and a welfare and health system that was increasingly dysfunctional.

The Western neo-liberal capitalism that had weakened the influence of government bureaucracies, at least inside the national economy, and had produced shrinking trade unions, unleashed a boom in the international economy in which the United States that was also propelled by the computer revolution and the dynamism of neo-liberal entrepreneurs in California and elsewhere. After the demise of the Soviet model, the United States figured very visibly as the No. 1 in the world economy. By the mid-1990s, this boom began to worry not only Clinton's critics, many of whom had remained Keynesians, but also Greenspan at the Federal Reserve. He spoke up against the 'irrational exuberance' in the stock market, implicitly warning that stocks could also be subject to slumps.[41] But neither Greenspan nor others in the Clinton and in the subsequent Bush administrations took action to put a damper on this exuberance. In 2007/8 the overvalued stock market promptly came crashing down. Although the banks received an enormous injection of cash from the U.S. Treasury in coordination especially with European treasuries to provide liquidity, Wall Street, London, Frankfurt and all financial centres were finally reminded that capitalism was a roller-coaster system. The weaknesses of neo-liberalism with its dismantling of the postwar welfare state now became so glaringly visible in the destitution and despair of millions of Americans, that this bleak picture gave rise to politicians, especially in Europe, who were glad that, while neo-liberal policies had also left their mark on the welfare support of the European Union, the dismantling of the 'social market economy' had never gone as far as in the United States and Britain.

They were supported by a number of historians and social scientists who began to point out that neo-liberalism had never completely swept the board and that there were in fact 'varieties of capitalism' waiting to be examined and tested to show that the American system, however pervasive, had always left enough room for alternative approaches to the running of a modern economy.[42] Accordingly, scholars no longer defined twenty-first century capitalism as a unitary system. They became interested in the study of the Swedish, German, Mediterranean, and even Chinese models. At the same time, other analysts focused on the impact of the digital revolution and what became called the 'platform capitalism' of giant corporations such as Amazon, Facebook, Google and Microsoft.[43] Their rise raised the question of whether we are again headed in the direction of monopolies. Yet, it seems that we are not quite back in the age of the Sherman Act which banned monopolies that were deemed to operate to the detriment of the consumer because of their ability to dictate prices. Jeff Bezos of Amazon.com claimed that, on the contrary, his corporation works for the benefit of the consumer, even if he himself has become one of the wealthiest entrepreneurs in the world at the same time. What is so intriguing about this 'platform capitalism' is that their quasi-monopoly positions have again raised the question of curbing their power. But what is so ironic about these developments is that the push for enforcement of anti-monopoly and anti-cartel rules has come in the first instance from the Europeans who, after 1945, took a long time to become convinced by American protagonists that oligopolistic competition rather than cartels and monopolies should be the structure of a socially responsible capitalism and its supervision and control by bureaucrats.

Returning to Max Weber and his conception of capitalism and bureaucracy a century ago, it is clear that some of his predictions about the rise of the *Fachmensch* who would dominate life on this planet have been quite accurate and are still of great concern to the future development of humanity and the planet, even if Weber only saw a few rays of hope for a future that left sufficient space for a creative individualism. This is why Mommsen's book on the 'Age of Capitalism and Bureaucracy' both of which Weber studied so intensively in his time is a worthwhile read even today.

Notes

1. Jürgen Kocka, *Unternehmensverwaltung und Angestelltenschaft am Beispiel Siemens*, 1847–1914, Stuttgart 1969.
2. Roger Chickering/Stig Förster, eds., *Great War, Total War*, Cambridge 2000.
3. Hilferding had completed this study in December 1909, and it was first published in 1913, before he reissued it under the same title in Vienna in 1923. Engl. translation: London 1981.
4. See, e.g., Hinnerk Bruhns, 'Un successo della pace durato? Max Weber nella guerra mondiale (A Long-Lasting Success of Peace? Max Weber in the World War)' in: *Scienza & Politica*, No. 63 (2020), 63–86. See also below p. 110 the discussion, in the 1970s, of what historians and social scientists then called 'Organized Capitalism' in an attempt to grapple with the evolution of Germany's political economy in World War I, also in comparative perspective.
5. See, e.g., Dietrich Geyer, *The Russian Revolution*, New York 1989. More narrowly focused: Rex A. Wade, *The Russian Revolution, 1917*, New York 2005.
6. On this power struggle and Stalin's eventual victory, followed by the creation of his ruthless dictatorship, see Sheila Fitzpatrick, *The Russian Revolution*, New York 2008; Stephen Kotkin, *Stalin*, New York 2014.
7. See, e.g., Carl P. Parini, *Heir to Empire. United States Economic Diplomacy*, 1916–1923, Pittsburgh 1969.
8. On Vanderlip and the larger context of US policy, see Volker Berghahn, *American Big Business in Britain and Germany. A Comparative History of Two 'Special Relationships' in the Twentieth Century*, Princeton 2014, 161ff.
9. See, e.g., *Woodrow Wilson and the Lost Peace*, Chicago 1944.
10. See, e.g., Margaret Macmillan, *Paris 1919. Six Months That Changed the World*, New York 2002.
11. See, e.g., Conan Fischer, *The Ruhr Crisis, 1923–1924*, New York 2003.
12. Still one of the best analysis, though never translated: Werner Link, *Die amerikanische Stabilisierungspolitik in Deutschland, 1921–1932*, Düsseldorf 1970. See also William McNeil, *American Money and the Weimar Republic*, New York 1986.
13. See, e.g., Mary Nolan, *Visions of Modernity. American Business and the Modernization of Germany*, New York 1994; Robert Lacey, *Ford. The Man and the Machine*, London 1987.
14. On the American principles of market organization see, e.g., Robert F. Himmelberg, *Business and Government in America since 1870*, Hamden, CT, 1994; Edward H. Chamberlin, ed., *Monopoly and Competition and Their Regulation*, New York 1954; Tony Freyer, *Regulating Big Business. Antitrust in Great Britain and America, 1880–1990*, Cambridge 1992.
15. John K. Galbraith, *The Great Crash, 1929*, Harmondsworth 1961, 103.
16. Galbraith (ibid., passim) also continues to be one of the best studies of the pre-1929 boom and the subsequent crash. See also Goronwy Rees, *The Great Slump. Capitalism in Crisis, 1929–1933*, London 1970.
17. See Robert Skidelsky, *Keynes*, Oxford 1996.
18. See, e.g., Alan Brinkley, *Franklin D. Roosevelt*, New York 2010; Carl N. Degler, ed., *The New Deal*, Chicago 1970.
19. See Berghahn (note 8), 245ff.
20. See, e.g., Adam Tooze, *Wages of Destruction. The Making and Breaking of the Nazi Economy*, New York 2006.
21. For the U.S. see, e.g., Walter Galenson, *The CIO Challenge to AFL. A History of the American Labor Movement, 1935–1941*, Cambridge, MA, 1960. For Nazi Germany, see, e.g., Ronald Smelser, *Robert Ley. Hitler's Labor Leader*, New York 1988.

22. See above p. 104.
23. New York 1941.
24. See, e.g., Victor Serge, *Life and Death of Leon Trotsky*, New York 1975.
25. See, e.g., Hans Pohl, ed., *Kartelle und Kartellgesetzgebung in Praxis und Rechtspre-chung vom 19. Jahrhundert bis zur Gegenwart*, Stuttgart 1985; Volker Hentschel, *Wirtschaft und Wirtschaftspolitik im Wilhelminischen Deutschland*, Stuttgart 1978.
26. On IG Farben see, e.g., Peter Hayes, *Industry and Ideology. IG Farben in the Nazi Era*, Cambridge 1987; Raymond Stokes, *Divide and Prosper. The Heirs of I.G. Farben under Allied Authority, 1945–1951*, Berkeley 1988, 3ff. On Vereinigte Stahl-werke see Alfred Reckendrees, *Das 'Stahltrust'-Projekt. Die Gründung der Verei-nigten Stahlwerke A.G. und die Unternehmensentwicklung, 1926–1933/34*, Munich 2000.
27. On Hitler's imperialist ambitions see Jochen Thies, *Hitler's Plans for Global Domi-nation*, New York 2012. See also Arno Sölter, *Grossraumkartell*, Dresden 1941.
28. Quoted in J. Davidow, 'The Seeking of a World Competition Code: Quixotic Quest?', in: Oscar Schachter/Robert Hellawell, eds., *Competition in International Business. Law and Policy on Restrictive Practices*, New York 1981, 361f.
29. On the origins of the Cold War see, e.g., Carole Fink, *Cold War. An International History*, Boulder, CO, 2017. For a classic study of the totalitarianism paradigm, though with a stronger emphasis on the Nazi model than the Stalnist one, see Hannah Arendt, *The Origins of Totalitarianism*, London 1951. On Vanderlip, see above, p. 101. On the Marshall Plan see, e.g., Michael Hogan, *The Marshall Plan. America, Britain and the Reconstruction of Western Europe, 1947–1952*, New York 1987; Benn Steil, *The Marshall Plan. Dawn of the Cold War*, New York 2018. Significant also the assessment that Dean Acheson provided in 1944, as quoted by John Eatwell, *Whatever Happened to Britain. The Economics of Decline*, Oxford 1982, 101f.: 'The United States has unlimited creative energy. The important thing is markets. We have got to see what the country produces is used and sold under financial arrangements which make its production possible . . . You must look to foreign markets. . . '.
30. See, e.g., Robert Schenkhan, *The Great Society*, New York 2017; Amity Slaes, *Great Society. A New History*, New York 2019.
31. See, e.g., Volker Berghahn, *The Americanisation of West German Industry, 1945–1973*, New York 1986, 302f.
32. See, e.g., William Diebold, *The Schuman Plan*, New York 1959; John Gillingham, *Coal, Steel and the Rebirth of Europe, 1945–1955*, Cambridge 1991.
33. See, e.g., Paul Addison, *The Road to 1945*, London 1994; T.D. Burridge, *Clement Attlee. A Political Biography*, London 1985.
34. See, e.g., James van Hook, R*ebuilding Germany. The Creation of the Social Market Economy, 1945–1957*, New York 2004.
35. For the origins of the 1951 law still unsurpassed: Gabriele Müller-List, ed., *Mon-tanmitbestimmung*, Düsseldorf 1984.
36. See, e.g., Judith Stein, *The Pivotal Decade. How the United States Traded Factories for Finance in the Seventies*, New Haven 2010.
37. See Heinrich-August Winkler, ed., *Organisierter Kapitalismus. Voraussetzungen und Anfänge*, Göttingen 1974.
38. See, e.g., Alan O. Ebenstein, *Milton Friedman. A Biography*, New York 2007; John C. Wood/Ronald N. Woods, *Milton Friedman. A Critical Assessment*, New York 1990; Tams K. Papp, *Tax Rate Cuts and Tax Compliance. The Laffer Curve Revis-ited*, Washington, D.C., 2002.
39. See, e.g., John Campbell, *Margaret Thatcher*, London 2000; John Blundell, *Mar-garet Thatcher. A Portrait of the Iron Lady*, New York 2008; Michael Schaller, *Ronald Reagan*, New York 2011.

40. See, e.g., Patrick Maney, *Bill Clinton. New Gilded Age President*, Lawrence, KS, 2016; Nigel Hamilton, *Mastering the Presidency*, New York 2007.
41. In his 'Age of Turbulence', New York 2007, 176, Alan Greenspan claimed to have invented the term. But it may have been the result of a conversation he had with the Yale University economist Robert Shiller who later published a bestseller: *Irrational Exuberance*, New York 2000.
42. See, e.g., Peter A. Hall, ed., *Varieties of Capitalism. The Institutional Foundations of Comparative Advantage*, New York 2001.
43. See K. S. Rahman/Katherine Thelen, 'Broken Contract: The Rise of the Networked Firm and the Transformation of 21st-Century Capitalism', CES Paper, Cambridge, MA, 2018.

Select Bibliography

Albrow, Martin, *Bureaucracy*, New York, 1970.
Appleby, Joyce, *The Relentless Revolution. A History of Capitalism*, New York, 2010.
Beckert, Sven, *Empire of Cotton. A Global History*, New York, 2014.
Bell, Daniel, *The Cultural Contradictions of Capitalism*, New York, 1979.
Bendix, Reinhard, *Max Weber. An Intellectual Portrait*, New York, 1960.
Blau, Peter, *Bureaucracy in Modern Society*, New York, 1987.
Braudel, Fernand, *Civilization and Capitalism, 15th–18th Century*, New York, 1982.
Chandler, Alfred D., *The Visible Hand. The Managerial Revolution in America*, Cambridge, MA, 1977.
———, *Scale and Scope. The Dynamics of Industrial Capitalism*, Cambridge, MA, 1990.
Eisenstadt, Stuart N., *The Protestant Ethic and Modernization*, New York, 1968.
——— (ed.), *Max Weber. On Charisma and Institution Building*, Chicago, 1968.
Giddens, Anthony, *Capitalism and Modern Social Theory*, Cambridge, 1971.
Gouldner, Alvin W., *Patterns of Industrial Bureaucracy*, New York, 1964.
Green, Rob W., *Protestantism and Capitalism. The Weber Thesis and Its Critics*, New York, 1959.
Hall, Peter A. and Soskice, David (eds), *Varieties if Capitalism*, Oxford, 2001.
Hobsbawm, Eric, *The Age of Capital*, London, 1975.
———, *The Age of Extremes, 1914–1991*, London, 1995.
Ingham, Geoffrey K., *Capitalism*, Cambridge, MA, 2008.
Kamenka, Eugene, *Bureaucracy*, Oxford, 1989.
Keynes, John M., *The General Theory of Employment, Interest and Money*, New York, 1936.
Kocka, Jürgen, *Capitalism. A Short History*, Princeton, 2014.
Kriedte, Peter, *Industrialization before Industrialization. Rural Industry in the Genesis of Capitalism*, New York, 1981.
———, *Peasants, Landlords and Merchant Capitalists. Europe and the World Economy, 1600–1800*, Leamington Spa, 1983.
Merton, Robert K., *Readings in Bureaucracy*, New York, 1967.
Muller, Jerry Z., *The Mind and the Market. Capitalism in Western Thought*, New York, 2005.
Piketty, Thomas, *Capital in the Twenty-First Century*, London, 2014.

Polanyi, Karl. *The Great Transformation. The Political and Economic Origins of Our Time*, Boston, 1944.

Rogers, Ralf E., *Max Weber's Ideal Type Theory*, New York, 1969.

Schumpeter, Joseph, *Capitalism, Socialism and Democracy*, London, 2006.

Shonfield, Andrew, *Modern Capitalism. The Changing Balance of Public and Private Power*, London, 1969.

Soros, George, *The Crisis of Global Capitalism*, New York, 1998.

Strange, Susan, *Casino Capitalism*, Manchester, 1997.

Streeck, Wolfgang, *Re-forming Capitalism. Institutional Change in the German Political Economy*, Oxford, 2009.

———, *How Will Capitalism End?*, London, 2016.

Tawney, Richard H., *Religion and the Rise of Capitalism*, Harmondsworth, 1964.

Wallerstein, Immanuel, *The Modern World System*, 4 vols, New York, 1974–2011.

———, *Historical Capitalism*, London, 1983.

Whitley, Richard (ed.), *Competing Capitalisms. Institutions and Economies*, Cheltenham, 2020.

Winkler, Heinrich-August (ed.), *Organisierter Kapitalismus. Voraussetzungen und Anfänge*, Göttingen, 1974.

Index

A

Alienation, 2, 47–49, 57, 84
Amazon, 113
Antoni, Carlo, 6, 19
Arendt, Hannah, 42, 115
Aron, Raymond, 24, 40, 75
Attlee, Clement, 109, 115
Austria-Hungary, 32–33

B

Baumgarten, Eduard, 22, 92
Bendix, Reinhard, 5, 19, 40, 58, 64, 75
Bezos, Jeff, 113
Big Bang, 111
Bildung, xiii, 52
Bismarck, Otto von, 40, 78–79
Bretton Woods, 110
British Empire, 109
Bukharin, Nicolai, 100
Bureaucracy, vi, xi–xiv, 1–4, 6, 8, 10, 12, 14, 16–18, 20, 24, 26, 28, 30, 32, 34, 36, 38, 40, 42, 44, 46, 48–50, 52–54, 56, 58, 62, 64–68, 70–72, 74, 76, 78–80, 82–84, 86–88, 90, 92, 98–106, 108–113
Burnham, James, 105

C

Capitalism, vi, ix–xiii, 2–4, 6–8, 10, 12–14, 16, 18, 20, 24, 26, 28, 30, 32, 34, 36–38, 40–42, 44, 46–59, 62, 64, 66, 68, 70, 72, 74, 76, 78, 80–84, 86, 88, 90, 92, 98–101, 103–114, 116

Cartel, 103, 106–107, 113
Carter, Jimmy, 110
Charisma, 3, 17–18, 64–65, 73–74, 82–83, 87, 89–90, 92
Christianity, 84, 91
Churchill, Winston, 73, 107
Class, viii–xi, xiii, 2, 10, 12, 24, 29, 34, 38, 43–45, 48–52, 56–58, 77–79, 84, 88, 90, 103, 105
Clayton Act, 103, 106–107
Clinton, William Jefferson, 112, 116
Co-determination, 110
Cold War, 107–109, 115

D

Dawes, Charles, 102
Delbrück, Hans, 28
Democracy, xiii, 3, 22–24, 60–61, 66–67, 70–74, 76, 80, 90–92
Dilthey, Wilhelm, 8
Disenchantment of the world, viii, 66, 91
Domination, vi, xi–xiii, 3, 15, 17–18, 55, 59–76, 90, 92, 108, 111, 115

E

Economy and Society, 7, 13–15, 17, 19–20, 42, 50, 54, 72
Eisenhower, Dwight D., 108
Eisner, Kurt, 73
Engels, Friedrich, 42, 44
Erhard, Ludwig, 42
European Coal and Steel Community, 109
European Union, 113

F
Fachmensch, 14, 113
Fascism, xiii, 102, 108
Ford, Henry, 102–103, 114
Francis, Emerich, 6–7, 19
Frankfurter Zeitung, 22
Freiburg, viii, 26, 42, 79, 87
Freyer, Hans, 41, 114
Friedman, Milton, 111, 115
Friedrich, Karl Joachim, 41–42, then
    Carl Joachim, 73

G
Galbraith, John K., 103, 114
German Empire, 34–35, 77
Gladstone, William, 73–74
Google, 113
Great Depression, 104, 109
Great Society, 108–110, 115
Greenspan, Alan, 112, 116

H
Hajek, Friedrich, 41
Hegel, Friedrich Wilhelm, ix, 6, 8, 44, 61
Herkner, Heinrich, 42
Herrschaft, xii, 15, 20, 65, 68, 75–76,
    105
Hilferding, Karl, 99, 114
Historical Materialism, 43, 45
Hitler, Adolf, viii, xiii, 24, 73, 102,
    104–108, 114–115
Honigsheim, Paul, 41, 58
Hoover, Herbert, 104

I
Ideal type, xi–xii, 9–10, 12–14, 16–17,
    43, 61
IG Farben, 106, 115
Imperial Chemical Industries, 106
Imperialism, 2, 22–25, 27–31, 33,
    35–39, 79

J
Japan, 104–105, 107
Jaspers, Karl, 22, 39, 41
Jellinek, Georg, 10, 81
Johnson, Lyndon, 108–110
Junker, 26, 29

K
Kamenev, Lev, 100
Kantianism, 8–9, 43
Kautsky, Karl, 44
Kennedy, John F., 108
Keynes, John Maynard, 103, 114
Kocka, Jürgen, 44, 58, 98, 114

L
Laffer, Arthur, 111, 115
League of Nations, 101
Lenin, Vladimir, 99–100
Levellers, 81, 85
Liberal Imperialism, 29
Liefmann, Robert, 88, 92
Löwenstein, Karl, 22, 39, 41, 73, 76
Löwith, Karl, 47–48, 57–58
Ludendorff, Erich, 31, 74, 102
Lukács, Georg, 41, 52
Lukes, Steven, xv
Luxemburg, Rosa, 36, 100

M
Machiavelli, Niccolo, 32, 61
Marcuse, Herbert, 2, 55–56, 59
Marshall, George F., 108, 115
Marxism, vi, ix–x, 3, 36, 42, 46, 58, 85,
    99, 105
Mason, Tim, xv
Mayer, Jacob Peter, 23, 40
Michels, Robert, 41, 70
Militarism, 102
Mill, John S., 23, 36, 40
Monopoly, xi, 37, 54–55, 78, 103,
    106–107, 113–114
Morgenthau, Henry, 104
Müller-Armack, Alfred, 42
Munich, xiii, 19, 46, 115
Mussolini, Benito, xiii

N
Nation, viii, x, 2, 23–37, 39, 71, 79, 87,
    90, 101, 104, 106, 110
National Health Service, 109
National Liberalism, 24, 78
National Socialism, xiii, 23
Naumann, Friedrich, 28
Neo-Liberalism, 111–113

New Deal, 104–105, 107, 109–110, 114
Nietzsche, Friedrich, 6, 9, 34, 43, 64, 75, 78, 83–86, 91–92
Nixon, Richard, 110

O
Oligopoly, 103, 106–107, 113
Open Door, 107, 109, 111
Organized Capitalism, 110, 114

P
Pacifism, 32
Palyi, Melchior, 22
Pan-German League, ix, 29–30
Parsons, Talcott, 5, 19, 41, 77, 91
Platform Capitalism, 113
Poles, 25–27, 30–31
Politics as a Vocation, 32, 72
Polonization, 25
Popper, Karl, 6
Power, vi–viii, x–xii, 2–3, 8, 22–25, 27–39, 41, 54, 56, 60, 67–68, 70–71, 73–76, 78–79, 81–82, 90–91, 98–100, 102, 105–106, 108–109, 111, 113–114
Protestant Ethic, x, xiii, 12, 44, 46–47, 81–82
Puritans, x, 81–82

R
Rationality, xiii, 2, 10, 17, 48, 53–56, 59, 73, 86
Rationalization, 7, 12, 17–18, 48, 52–53, 56, 65–66, 80, 82–83, 85–86, 89–90
Reagan, Ronald, 111–112, 115
Reichstag, 30–31
Rex, John, 6, 19, 114
Ricardo, David, 36
Richter, Melvin, xv
Rickert, Heinrich, 8–10
Rieff, Philip, xv
Roman Empire, 7–8, 39, 80, 90
Roosevelt, Franklin D., 73–74, 104–107, 112, 114
Roscher, Wilhelm, 61
Russia, ix, 30, 35, 80, 99–100

S
Schlesinger, Arthur, Jr., 73, 76
Schmitt, Carl, 9, 41
Schumpeter, Joseph, 36–37, 41
Serfdom, vii, xii, 14, 48, 81, 105
Sherman Act, 113
Simey, T.S., 87, 92
Slave labour, 7
Social Darwinism, 28
Socialism, xiii, 23, 41–42, 44–46, 49, 53–54, 56–58, 84–85, 110
Sölter, Arno, 106, 115
Sombart, Werner, 42, 81
Soviet Union, 100, 104–105
Stalin, Josef, 100, 105–107, 114
Stammler, Rudolf, 42, 46
Switzerland, 33–34

T
Thatcher, Margaret, 111, 115
Tolstoy, Leo, 32
Toynbee, Arnold, 6
Treaty of Brest-Litovsk, ix
Trotsky, Leon, 100, 105, 115

U
United States, x, xiii, 31, 35, 42, 100–101, 103–110, 112–115

V
Vanderlip, Frank, 101, 108, 114–115
Vereinigte Stahlwerke, 106, 115

W
Wall Street, 101, 111–112
Weber, Marianne, xiii
Weimar, 22–24, 99, 106, 110, 114
Weltanschauung, 44
Weltpolitik, 28
Wilhelm II, viii, 22
Wilson, Woodrow, 31, 101–102, 114
World Exhibition, x

Z
Zaibatsu, 106
Zinoviev, Alexander, 100

CPSIA information can be obtained
at www.ICGtesting.com
Printed in the USA
BVHW041412230621
610290BV00014B/350